God Help Us!

God Help Us!

The Bible and Pastoral Care Concerns for Black Churches

Edited by

Raynard D. Smith
Terry Ann Smith

the pilgrim press

The Pilgrim Press, 1300 East 9th Street
Cleveland, Ohio 44114
thepilgrimpress.com

Published 2025.

Library of Congress Cataloging-in-Publication Data on file.
LCCN: 2024950009

ISBN 978-0-8298-0314-3 (paper)
ISBN 978-0-8298-2245-8 (ebook)

Typeset in Freight Text, Freight Sans, and Aesthet Nova.

Printed on acid-free paper in the United States of America.

Contents

Preface

God Help Us! is a bold witness of the significance of the Black Church and the strength of Black people against all odds. From the establishment of the thirteen British colonies, which eventually became the United States of America, people of African descent were legally prevented from receiving a formal education. The restriction on educating our people was in effect between 1619 until the end of the American Civil War in 1865, with lingering negative impacts on our society today.

At the end of the American Civil War in 1865, most predominately white institutions (PWIs), including seminaries largely ignored Black people and did not consider the Black Church an institution that could be systematically equipped for ministry.

Fortunately, it was at this time God provided visionaries and pathways for the creation of historically Black theological institutions (HBTIs). We are grateful that many of the HBTIs started in the 1800s continue to faithfully serve the Black Church and Black people today. The HBTIs help prepare clergy, laity, and theologians to support communities of color in overcoming obstacles steeped in racial discrimination that continue to cause trauma, depression, fragmented families, loneliness, and imprisonment of Black men and Black women.

God Help Us! provides numerous examples to encourage the reader to explore biblical interpretations and pastoral care practices to help us cope with daily living. This resource inspires us to achieve and strive for greatness despite our past and present obstacles. This text is essential for all who desire to acknowledge and contend with discrepancies, deficits, and dilemmas within congregational life that have often been ignored.

Thankfully, *God Help Us!* focuses on all of God's children with special emphasis on Black People. This book represents the necessary but rare academic courage to discuss the Black Church in real-life terms. The authors have chosen to venture into spheres of theological scholarship focusing on God's children, from the perspective of Black fathers, Black mothers, Black children, and beyond. I hope you read, reflect, and refocus for the journey!

Grace and Peace,

Rev. Dr. Ken Walden

Senior Pastor of Holman United Methodist Church (Los Angeles, California), Former President-Dean of Gammon Theological Seminary (Atlanta, Georgia)

Introduction

The sacred text of the Christian tradition is replete with narratives that speak to a wide array of social, physical, and psychological concerns encompassing the human condition. When read through the lens of the Black experience, these stories not only serve as guidance for faith formation but also serve as points of reflexivity and action on the myriad concerns faced by this group (grief, depression, immigration, single parenting, etc.).[1] Whether during Sunday morning worship or midweek Bible study, Black pastors seek to relate biblical narratives to the experiences and contexts of those in their congregations. Operating within the African indigenous oral tradition of the griot (the village storyteller), pastors bring to life the biblical text for Black people whose history is one of oppression and exploitation.[2] Colonization and systemic structural racism by the dominant society have left their marks on Black people, where the lingering effects of intergenerational trauma have produced the vast majority of problems that congregants experience. This, in turn, impacts how they interact in their homes, their communities, and society at large. This volume gathers a collection of essays that integrate interpretative readings of the Bible with practical theology. John Swinton and Harriet Mowat define practical theology as critical theological reflection on the practices of the church as they interact with the practices of the world with a view to ensuring and enabling faithful participation in God's redemptive practices into and for the world.[3] We, the editors, assume this definition as a lens that gives focus to the chapters. Here, the application of the social sciences with selective practical pastoral care issues pertinent to Black Church congregations offers a prescription for addressing these concerns. Our colleagues join us in this creative literary endeavor. These essays encompass the lived experiences of some (not all) Black Americans and include but are not limited to the topics of depression, grief, traumatic loss and reconciliation, mass incarceration, female advocacy and agency, African migration, and Black males and fatherlessness. Each essay in this volume focuses on a biblical text read in tandem with a contemporary social issue and concludes with questions that allow the reader to further explore the text or the issue under consideration.

In chapter 1, "The Mourning After: Leah, Loss and Depression in Genesis 29," Raynard Smith and Terry Smith explore Leah's emotional state as she names her children, suggesting she suffers from dysthymia, a chronic form of depression, the result of her unrequited love for Jacob. The authors then connect Leah's experience to rising depression rates among women, particularly single African American women who desire a marriage partner. They emphasize the need for Black churches to address mental health issues. They advocate for increased awareness, hope, and pastoral care interventions for women suffering from depression.

In chapter 2, "Migratory Grief and Cultural Melancholia among African Immigrants in the United States: Insights for Pastoral Care and Counseling, Genesis 11–25," Fulgence Nyengele examines the biblical immigration story of Abraham in Genesis 12 and in subsequent chapters. He draws parallels to the experience of African immigrants to highlight some major issues immigrants typically encounter in the United States. He identifies grief and loss as a significant psychological dynamic taking place in the lived experiences of African immigrants as they seek to acclimate themselves to their new American environment. He urges churches to be aware of these struggles and provide necessary support for immigrants in their communities.

In chapter 3, "All God's Children: Grief as a Reconciliatory Agent in 2 Samuel 21:1–14," Terry Smith and Micah McCreary analyze the story of David's execution of Saul's seven sons and the silent vigil of one grieving mother, Rizpah. They draw parallels between Rizpah's vigil and modern cries for justice from mothers who have lost children due to systemic disparities and biases in our political, economic, and justice systems. The chapter explores the impact of cultural, psychosocial, and spiritual factors on trauma and emphasizes grief and trauma as crucial pastoral care concerns.

In chapter 4, "Restoring the Fathers, Saving Our Sons: An Empathic Reading of Jephthah's Vow in Judges 11:30–31," Raynard Smith focuses on Jephthah's vow in Judges 11:30–31 as a classic example of zealous desire to meet a psychological need derived from an unmet desire for acceptance and belonging, which ideally is the normal psychological nurturance exhibited in healthy African American families. Jephthah's story, as the rejected brother and son presumably raised singularly by his mother, finds resonance with the lived experience of many African American males raised in a single-parent home where the mother is the sole caregiver. Churches that seek to address the issue of fatherlessness and its impact upon African American families must engage with how the existential experience of fatherlessness may undergird some (not all) negative behaviors that emerge in African American males (youth and adults). This would call for initiatives that discuss loss and foster forgiveness, which might result in African American male children becoming receptive to the creation of new, life-affirming relational bonds established through mutual trust with mentors from father-like or other figures placed in their lives.

In chapter 5, "Nurturing the Disruptive Voice: Reflections on Naaman's Slave Girl (2 Kings 5) and Cultivating the Voices of African American and Afro-Caribbean Immigrant Girls," Janice McLean-Farrell and Terry Smith examine how Naaman's unnamed slave girl illustrates the potential of young voices to challenge the status quo. We propose that the slave girl's response to her oppressor's predicament can inspire Black girls to recognize, embrace, and use their voices to challenge Western stereotypes that portray their assertiveness negatively. We submit that silencing African American and Black immigrant girls can lead to diminished self-confidence. We also argue that Black churches must adopt new parenting and mentoring approaches to prepare and empower these young girls for the future ahead of them.

Finally, in chapter 6, "'He Ain't Heavy, He's My Brother': Rereading Genesis 39–41 through the Lens of Mass Incarceration," Raynard Smith explores the narrative of Joseph's imprisonment in Genesis 39–41 and the high incidence of Black males entangled in the American criminal justice system. The comparison presents an opportunity for Black churches to engage in critical reflection and social and political engagement on the issue of mass incarceration, its toll on African American males, and the collateral damage caused to the Black family. Like the imprisoned Joseph, African American incarcerated males are absent from their families, an absence that directly affects their children, spouses, mothers, fathers, sisters, brothers, and significant others who are left to deal with the severance of emotional bonds, which may engender grief, anger, separation, and shame. Black churches can serve as repairers of the breach, partnering with community social agencies in providing support to returning citizens. If Black churches take a part in the restorative and redemptive process of returning citizens, their participation has the potential to aid in the reduction of recidivism among this population.

Overall, we hope these intersectional examinations and interpretations of biblical texts together with reflections on contemporary contexts that embody the Black experience provide Black pastors with new insights for integrating scripture into social justice advocacy. By engaging these topics, it is our desire to stimulate conversations among pastors, lay leaders, and teachers in Black churches as well as seminarians and professors in academic communities. We hope these conversations bring awareness to human situations while fostering strategic interventions for the necessary liberatory praxis of ministry.

Endnotes

1 Here, we use the term Black to refer to African Americans, Afro-Caribbeans, and African immigrants.

2 Edward Wimberly identifies the preaching tradition inherent in Black churches as extending back to slavery where it was cultivated as a source for healing and empowerment. See *African American Pastoral Care and Counseling* (Abingdon Press, 2008), 28–29.

3 John Swinton and Harriet Mowat, *Practical Theology and Qualitative Research* (SCM Press, 2016), 7.

1

The Mourning After: Leah, Loss and Depression in Genesis 29

Raynard D. Smith
and Terry Ann Smith

This chapter examines the family dynamics undergirding the story of Leah and Rachel in Genesis 29. Specifically, it proposes that Leah likely suffers from dysthymia, a mild and persistent form of depression, the result of her inability to gain the object of her desire and affection, Jacob. We further suggest that evidence of Leah's sickened state is most observable in the naming of her children. For example, Genesis 29:32 associates Reuben with affliction, while Simeon is linked with hatred in 29:33.

> So Jacob went into Rachel also, and he loved Rachel more than Leah. He served Laban for another seven years. When the Lord saw that Leah was unloved, he opened

> her womb, but Rachel was barren. Leah conceived and bore a son, and she named him Reuben, for she said, "Because the Lord has looked on my affliction, surely now my husband will love me." She conceived again and bore a son and said, "Because the Lord has heard that I am hated, he has given me this son also," and she named him Simeon (Genesis 29:30–33).

The story of Leah—the unfavored daughter and less favored wife—can be fruitfully read together with the rising rate of depression among women in general and single African American women in particular. This interpretation points to the need for a heightened conversation within Black churches regarding circumstances, symptoms, and self-care for those dealing with this mental disorder. The pastoral implications suggest the need for engendering hope and healing when ministering to women who suffer from this malady of the soul, often in silence.

Sins of the Family

The patriarchal narratives begin in Genesis 12. God calls Abraham to sever his kinship ties and abandon his homeland. In an act of faith, he sets out with his barren wife Sarah toward the unknown (Canaan). In their later years, this elderly couple will have a son, the promised one, Isaac; however, not before Sarah takes matters into her own hands and a son is born to Abraham and Sarah's handmaid, Hagar (Genesis 16 and 21). Sometime later, Isaac is almost offered up on Mount Moriah when the combined arrival of "an angel of the Lord" and a lamb in a bush miraculously saves the day (Genesis 22). Following this potentially traumatic experience, Isaac will wed Rebekah who gives birth to the fraternal twins Esau and Jacob (Genesis 25). With the aid of his mother, Jacob will emerge with Esau's birthright and blessing, a costly deception that forces him to flee his home to escape Esau's wrath (Genesis 27). Jacob's journey takes him to Paddan-Aram, the home of his mother's father, where he is to obtain a wife from one of the daughters of his mother's brother, Laban (Genesis 28).

Our analysis of these events begins in Genesis 29 at the local well, where Jacob first encounters one of Laban's daughters. In the biblical narrative, the well has a multitude of functions, ranging from a landmark on routes between ancient settlements (for instance, Numbers 21:16, Deuteronomy 10:6, Judges 9:16–21) to a place for negotiating important contracts and agreements (Genesis 26:31). As an open place where people gathered, wells also served as the hot spot for meeting one's future spouse.[1] Laban's daughter Rachel arrives at this place of potential romance to water her father's flocks. Jacob's overwhelming reaction to her is evident as he, not the men of the village, rolls the stone away from the well opening. It is he, not Rachel, who attends to the business of watering her sheep. The encounter concludes with his kiss, his cries, and his announcement of their kinship connections (Genesis 29:11–12). Jacob sees this young woman at the well and it is love at first sight, so much so that he is willing to work not seven but fourteen years for her, the object of his desire (Genesis 29:18, 27 and 28). What is it about Rachel that has Jacob so drawn to her? According to the text, Rachel has beauty, favor, and thus the opportunity to attract and perhaps gain the love of a good man (Genesis 29:17 and 18).

Unlike the beautiful Rachel, the Torah provides no physical description of Leah with the exception of her eyes, which are described with the Hebrew term *rak*. The exact meaning of *rak* as used in 29:17 remains unclear. The NRSV translates it as "lovely," while the Tanakh and NAS render it as "weak." Amy Kalmanofsky asserts, "However one understands the term 'weak eyes,' it is a physical contrast between the two sisters."[2] Talmudic and Midrashic sources suggest that descriptors such as "weak" or "lackluster" capture Leah's response to her external circumstances, which resulted from her prolonged weeping over an arranged marriage between herself and Jacob's brother Esau.[3] This explanation of Leah's saddened state counters the biblical portrayal of one whose own father, according to L. Daniel Hawk, "apparently cannot obtain a husband for Leah apart from subterfuge."[4] Still, scholars like Seelenfreund and

Schneider suggest that the terms "weak" and "lackluster" should not be viewed as "a negative description of Leah's appearance, but rather a statement of how she *made* herself look because of her crying."[5] The rendering of *rak* as "lackluster" has important implications for our reading of Genesis 29. When juxtaposed with Israelite concepts of beauty (Genesis 12:11, 39:6; 1 Samuel 25:3; 2 Samuel 14:25–26; Esther 2:7), it is instructive that the narrator emphasizes Leah's eyes as her most striking feature, eyes that fail to exhibit a certain vibrancy or brilliancy when *rak* is translated as "lackluster."[6] There is a well-used saying that "the eyes are the window to the soul." This implies that one's eyes can provide valuable information concerning an individual's health and emotional state. If Leah's eyes, as the text suggests, "lack luster," then it is likely that the sparkle that typically accompanies a healthy emotional state is gone. Given this, is it possible that Leah's countenance indicates that something is awry? In other words, can we associate *rak* with a demeanor that suggests a woman troubled by her circumstances? Is it possible that her appearance is evidence of a person suffering from dysthymia—a persistent low-grade depressive state?

According to the Diagnostic and Statistical Manual for Mental Disorders 5 (DSM5) criteria, dysthymia or persistent depressive disorder (PDD) is characteristic of 1) a lasting sad, anxious, or empty mood; 2) lessened ability to concentrate, think, and/or make decisions; 3) lessened energy; 4) fatigue; 5) feeling of hopelessness; 6) weight gain or loss due to either overeating or under eating; 7) changes is sleep pattern, insomnia or oversleeping; and 8) low self-esteem. For an individual to be diagnosed with PDD, they would have to exhibit a depressed mood for at least two weeks along with at least two of these symptoms.[7]

Dysthymia is a variation of depression. Depression as a mood disorder is commonly known to manifest itself in a person(s) experiencing extreme stressful and/or debilitating events, as in the case of loss (real or imagined), be it of a loved one, a position, or any other attachment (animate or inanimate) in which one has deposited a significant emotional investment.[8] The person unable or unwilling to adjust to the new reality without the desired object internalizes the "loss" as frustration and anger.[9] Finding themselves in a less than desirable environment and unable to express their true feelings of anger and frustration causes these feelings to be directed inward, after which they may lead to a depressed state over time.[10] One way in which this internalized loss might be externally manifested is found in the depressed person's sense of self-worth and self-esteem.

Psychodynamic Perspective

In his seminal essay "Mourning and Melancholia," Sigmund Freud examined the psychic dynamics of grief and depression, which he called melancholia—a severe form of depression. He noted the similarities as well as the distinctions between normal grief due to the loss of a desired love object and depression. He contended that both mourning and depression are "regularly the reaction to the loss of a loved person, or to the loss of some abstraction which has taken the place of one, such as fatherland, liberty, an ideal, and so on".[11] Freud further delineated the following concerning melancholia:

> The distinguishing mental features of melancholia are a profoundly painful dejection, abrogation of interest in the outside world, loss of the capacity to love, inhibition of all activity, and a lowering of the self-regarding feelings to a degree that finds utterance in self-reproaches and self-revilings, and culminates in a delusional expectation of punishment.[12]

Freud asserted that notwithstanding lowered self-esteem, grief and melancholia exhibit similar symptomatology. For him, grief is a normal response to loss and follows a course called mourning in which a person seeks to adjust to a life without the object. Melancholia, in contrast, is a profound state of sadness that affects one interpersonally, physiologically, cognitively, and behaviorally, and usual requires professional assistance.

The outward manifestation of this particular state of sadness is typically referred to as depression and can range from mild to moderate to severe. Reflecting on women specifically, Susan Dunlap critiques Freud's approach (while acknowledging his contribution to our understanding of depression), especially since Freud tended to pathologize women's experience.[13] She correctly notes that Freud's theorizing gives sole attention to the intrapsychic dimensions of depression while neglecting to engage with the external cultural context.[14] This is an important observation because it is this environment that impacts the lived experience of women. Second, she contends that Freud gives no consideration to the ways in which interpersonal power dynamics between men and women influence the lived experience of women.[15] And third, she asserts, the psychodynamic approach by its very nature of being insight oriented tends to take more of a passive role in its treatment of depression.[16] Christie Cozad Neuger offers that depression is "more common in women, people with inadequate financial resources, and people without adequate relational support."[17] Moreover, dysthymia, as a milder yet chronic form of depression, consistently appears as a "personality trait rather than a form of depression" and thus is easily overlooked or labeled as something else.[18]

Genesis 29 says nothing about how Leah and Rachel interacted with one another prior to meeting Jacob. Yet, there is reason to surmise that Leah had lived in the shadows of her younger sister's beauty and possibly her father's favoritism for quite some time, if biblical motifs that depict preferential treatment for the younger sibling over the older one are equally applicable here (Rebekah/Jacob, Jacob/Joseph). Drawing upon the work of psychologist Walter Toman, Ronald Richardson offers a theoretical construction of the characteristics and significance of birth order on sibling behavior.[19] When applied to Genesis, his conclusions suggest that Leah, as the eldest sister, would have been destined to be the leader. Her parents would have instructed her on the need to set an example for other siblings.

This expectation would have endowed Leah with such qualities as being the most knowledgeable and comfortable with "leading, directing, guiding, and helping," making her the most responsible of all their children.[20]

On the other hand, Rachel as the youngest daughter would likely have developed a personality of being free-spirited, "hyper-feminized" in the sense of appearing to be flirtatious as well as competitive. Richardson states, "Her competitive side may come out with women, where she is seen wanting to have more, sooner, of whatever is valued in her group of friends, be it marriage, children, material goods, or whatever."[21] This potentially explains the rivalry between Leah and Rachel, which might have manifested early in their lives.[22] This rivalry, together with the entrance of Jacob into the family dynamic, serves as a major trigger that could contribute to Leah's overall demeanor. Leah's lackluster eyes, as representative of her emotional state, alert us to the fact that something is terribly amiss in this woman's world. We read of no "well" encounters for Leah, no access and exposure to that one man that might result in the matrimonial bliss that will come so readily to her sister. If God noticed that Leah was unloved (Genesis 29:31), was it because no one else had noticed her or is God complicit in her sufferings? In her assessment of the relational dynamics attending this story, Renita Weems writes, "No pain is more poignant and deafening than the pain that comes in relationships."[23] Leah's pain is tripartite. There is the psychological trauma of dealing with the betrayal of her father.[24] As Carolyn Helsel and Song-Mi Suzie Park astutely observe, it was her father's actions that instigated the problem. His actions placed her in the middle of a tangled relational web: married to a husband who spent his waking moments wishing she were someone else, and a sister whose very presence was the someone else?[25]

Again, Freud posited that whereas one who mourns takes the lost object into their self-structure, for the melancholic there is an ambiguity in relation to the lost object.[26] The object is perceived—whether consciously or unconsciously—as having abandoned the individual and is thus criticized and "hated."[27] Instead of the lost object losing emotional significance and being diminished, gradually subsiding over time, it continues to hold sway over the individual. Thus, the lost object is absorbed into the ego and then becomes the target of anger and harmful thoughts directed against the self. This engenders recriminating thoughts about the self and against the self, when repressed, can predispose the individual to a sunken state of depression. Neuger writes, "Depression is a total experience. It involves the mind, the spirit, the body, important relationships, casual relationships, work, family, leisure time, and so on. There is no aspect that depression leaves untouched when it enters a person's life."[28] Is it possible that the pain Leah cannot name or openly express finds resonance in the names she chooses for her children and serves as further evidence of her sullen emotional state?

The preponderance of evidence in the Hebrew Bible suggests that children received their names from their mothers more often than from their fathers.[29] While naming points to the important role that women played in individual households, it also simultaneously conveyed their hopes, aspirations, and despair. In naming her first three children, Leah expresses her distress over her loveless marriage. The eldest son, Reuben (which means "behold a son"), receives his name because God saw that Leah was unloved. Leah's desire to obtain the object of her affection, Jacob, is captured by the words "surely now my husband will love me." This desire seemingly reflects her grief and sorrow regarding the lack of relationship between the two and the hope of gaining his admiration (Genesis 29:32). By gaining her husband's admiration, Leah can buoy up her low self-esteem. The birth and naming of the second son Simeon (a play on the Hebrew word *shama*, meaning to hear or listen) suggest the growing fragility of their marital bonds, as Leah's despair is heard for a second time in her declaration that "the LORD heard that she was hated" (Genesis 29:33). Whether the culprit is Jacob or her sister Rachel (or both), we might imagine it lends nothing to this woman's self-esteem but adds to her anguish and sadness.

Leah's womb may produce sons, but Jacob does not appear to "cleave" any closer to her because of this. The futility of Leah's efforts and her mounting frustration is cataloged further with the naming of her third child Levi (possibly meaning attached) as she still longs to be "joined" to her husband (Genesis 29:34). Wilma Bailey submits that Leah is bearing children for herself and that the naming does not reflect "expressions of complaint, sorrow or grief."[30] Yet, Leah's rationale for naming her children is a clear indication of her clouded inner emotional state. She is caught up in a tangled web of patriarchy and sibling rivalry in which her desire to be the object of Jacob's affection continues to go unheeded. Each birth poses the question as to whether Leah experiences the intrinsic joy that most mothers experience when holding their newborn son or daughter. For her, this joy is eclipsed by the stark reality that she is still unloved. She is disappointed repeatedly because the birth of a male child has not brought about what she wanted most—the affection of Jacob, the desired object.

The commentary following the naming of these children suggests that Leah is failing in her efforts to make this occur. Thus, Leah's lament of loneliness, reflected in the rationale behind her children's names, cannot be dismissed so easily. How does one deal with the pain of rejection, not once, but three times? Leah's story involves a husband who seemingly is indifferent to her feelings and a sister who will envy her apparent fecundity (Genesis 30:1). Leah raises her laments to the only one in the text who cares enough to collaborate with her in her sorrow, her God.[31] Hawk submits that "God intervenes on behalf of one who, up to this point, has had no say in the fundamental decisions that affect her" and that "we begin to realize the depth of her longing and isolation as well as the comfort she now takes in knowing that the LORD cares for her."[32]

The naming of the fourth son Judah (meaning "praise") suggests that something has changed for Leah. Has she completed the mourning process in which her grief and sorrow over not becoming the preferred object of Jacob's desire are concluded?[33]

In other words, realizing the continued futility of her efforts, has Leah adjusted to life as Jacob's second wife and decided to move on? Here, the naming of her fourth son may represent Leah's way of re-interpreting her situation, now viewed as a life filled with potential and promise. Still, such a rendering may be a bit premature. Genesis 29:35 states that Leah "ceased" bearing children, a cessation most likely brought about because Jacob has now obtained the object of his affection (i.e., Rachel) and thus has "ceased" sleeping with Leah.

Moreover, despite having several sons, the text depicts an ever-increasing rivalry between Leah and Rachel. With the offering of her handmaid, we possibly witness a desperate attempt by Leah to prove that she is (or could be) the better choice, since the handmaid as an extension of Leah's womb also produces two sons, Gad (meaning good fortune) and Asher (meaning happy one). Like the birth of Ishmael in Genesis 16:2, Gad and Asher seemingly represent an attempt to build Leah up. As she already has four sons, we can surmise that somehow Leah still feels inadequate. Here, the underlying rationale behind the naming of Gad and Asher represents how she wants others to perceive her—namely, as a happy woman (Genesis 30:11–13). But at the same time, it implies the opposite—a woman whose unhappiness remains unabated. That she barters with Rachel for a single night with Jacob in Genesis 30:15 says much about the fluctuation of Leah's state of mind. Clearly, the normative detachment that accompanies the mourning process suggests that Leah has not let go of her hopes regarding Jacob, a point further evinced in the naming of her last two sons, Issachar and Zebulun. As in the births of her previous sons, Leah acknowledges the deity's role in the birth of these children, but she nonetheless continues to hold Jacob in sight as the object of her musings. We can almost hear her wearied sigh, "now my husband will honor me" (Genesis 30:20) after the birth of Zebulun.

Having failed to secure Jacob's love, she holds out hope that somehow he will value her for the fruits of her loins. Terrance Fretheim suggests "the word plays on the children's names are not really etymologies but reflections on the familial conflict and God's action thereto."[34] Perhaps, what Leah has been denied in life, she ultimately achieves in death. In Genesis 49:31, we learn that Jacob is laid to rest next to Leah, rather than Rachel. Whether one views this as the logical outcome for this couple (Rachel precedes them both with her death while giving birth to Benjamin), we (and maybe the narrator of the Genesis story) would like to imagine that Leah's eyes regained their luster.

Depression among Black Women

Leah's struggle to secure the affections of Jacob and the contentions with her sister theoretically read as triggers for a low-grade depressive disposition, which lends itself to a larger discussion of depression in women in general. This is not to suggest that depression does not occur among men. However, studies on depression indicate that women are much more prone to depression than men.[35] Neuger attributes this to the culture of patriarchy and incidences of traumatic aggression arising from physical or sexual abuse.[36] While depression can be defined in a myriad of ways and result from a variety of external factors, the major culprit in Genesis 29 appears to be the marital relationship. Leah's marital relationship can best be described as one that causes her much dissatisfaction, for although married to Jacob, she is not the preferred wife. According to pastoral theologian Howard Stone, people who experience marital problems are predisposed to depression. He contends, "If a woman sees her marriage as unsatisfactory, she has as much as a one-to-two chance of being depressed."[37] Neuger nuances this further, stating, "When women feel relatively powerless . . . in a marriage relationship, which exists in a larger culture also working to disempower her, they are more likely to become depressed."[38] It is clear from the text that Leah's marital conflict exemplified in her rivalry with her sister, Rachel, causes her great consternation and would only compound her already depressed state. Arguably, the text does not speak of a condition. However, it does present a dilemma where Leah's suffering is voiced through the naming of her children. Thus, the text affords Leah an agency that most women suffering from depression do not have given the cultural stigma associated with depression. This is especially true among African Americans, who for quite a while "characterized depression as a 'White disease' and viewed it as a sign of personal weakness."[39]

Like their white counterparts, Black women are more likely than Black men to have a depressive episode.[40] While we recognize that within Black churches there is heterogeneity among Black women, which would cause us to be cautious about overgeneralizing, for some single Black women, the experience of depression brought on by their desire for marriage may be more prevalent than imagined. A study by John Cacioppo and others reports a correlation between loneliness and depression, arguing that "situational factors can increase the frequency or chronicity of loneliness."[41] According to Akiim DeShay, African American women are the least likely of women of any other ethnic group to get married.[42] In 2010, 45.2% of African American women were single or unwed, a number that by 2020 had increased to 48.0% and continues to grow. The reason behind the increase in single or unwed African American women is in part due to social factors that affect the number of eligible African American males (mass incarceration, un- or under-employment, violence, substance abuse, lack of education, homicide, etc.). Moreover, since the majority of African American females prefer endogamous marriages (i.e., marriage to an African American male), the failure to find an eligible marriage partner only increases the likelihood that they will remain single.[43] Consequently, in a culture that highly celebrates marriage and the nuclear family, her occasions and experiences of loneliness may be profoundly pronounced, and thus her depressive episodes may occur more frequently yet go unnoticed. Some single African American women may be sexually active and have children but not be connected to long-lasting meaningful partnerships.[44] This absence and strong desire for relationships may predispose them to suffer from dysthymia. One could posit that similar to Leah, who was unable to obtain the object of her affection, these women are unable to obtain the object of their desire, marriage to a Black man, a situation that for them presents itself as a frequent and unending problem.[45]

Another factor that contributes to depression among African American women is what Walker-Barnes critiques as the myth of the "StrongBlackWoman." Conceived as a model of strength, women striving to adhere to the model "rely upon defense mechanisms of repression and suppression to deal with negative emotions."[46] Walker-Barnes argues, "While limited use of defense mechanisms such as denial, repression, and suppression can be an effective means to cope with stressful situations temporarily, long-term reliance upon them is a guaranteed recipe for emotional and physical overload."[47] In other words, it is a guaranteed recipe for having a number of depressive episodes or worse an emotional or physical breakdown.

Unlike their white counterparts, many Black women have had to contend with the triple oppressions of sexism, racism, and classism that abound within the larger society. The poverty rate within the Black community impacts the lives of Black women and children at an alarming rate. BlackDemographics.com documents that "according to the 2014 U.S. Census Bureau ACS study, 27% of all African American men, women and children live below the poverty level, compared to just 11% of all Americans. The effects of poverty upon the Black psyche are immense."[48]

Given this information, Sunday morning worship services in Black Churches, where women tend to outnumber Black men, could be filled with women who may be struggling with persistent depressive disorder. They may exhibit a variety of symptoms such as "depressed mood lasting at least two or more years, poor or excessive appetite, insomnia or hypersomnia, low energy or fatigue, low self-esteem, poor concentration or being indecisive about making important decisions, and feelings of hopelessness."[49] In addition, while many of these women may be functioning—caring for parents, children, spouses, and lovers, working jobs, pursuing careers, continuing education—these same women experience a continuous feeling of disenchantment and despair and little to no joy. To quote Terrie Williams, "it just looks like we're not hurting, it's not just what we say, it's about what we don't say."[50] The StrongBlackWoman presents a face of invulnerability; thus, most view her suffering as normal. She is like the Timex slogan, "takes a licking and keeps on ticking." She is the poster child for black femininity. Her image has come to characterize and dominate "the worldviews, behaviors, thoughts, and feelings of African American women, shaping how they perceive and interact with the world."[51] These same women (many of them single) may sit in congregations, suffering in silence, struggling with a persistent low-grade depressive condition. Dysthymia leaves them functioning and passing not as normal women, but as superwomen who sacrifice health and emotional well-being for the sake of an image.

Black Church Response

The potentially devastating long-term effects of undiagnosed and untreated depression pose serious health concerns for individuals and their interpersonal relationships. Given that the majority of Black church congregations consist predominantly of Black women, the following suggestions offer ways that pastoral care initiatives can aid in addressing depression within Black church congregations and thus engendering hope and healing. While these suggestions are not exhaustive, they might serve as a beginning for Black churches seeking to address important issues relative to the lives of their constituents, and particularly single women with or without children.

First, it is incumbent upon pastors and leadership in Black churches to recognize and acknowledge that dysthymia is a major issue that can be camouflaged as normalcy among African Americans. According to Anahvia Taiyib Mewborn, African Americans experience high incidences of what she describes as cultural dysthymia, which is precipitated by the impact of systemic oppression compounded by poverty.[52] She states,

> Among African Americans, racism has been identified as the number one most prevalent and most potent cause of psychological distress. Since racism and poverty are inextricably linked, African Americans experience more than just "pure" race-based discrimination; being Black in America precipitates and exacerbates mental illness. Cultural dysthymia is a form of persistent depressive disorder (PDD; dysthymia) that is precipitated and exacerbated by racial discrimination. Symptoms include chronic depressed mood and anger or hostility, especially when in interpersonal conflicts with a member of a privileged group.[53]

Noting the prevalence of mental health issues among African Americans due to racial trauma, Black psychologists Jessica Young Brown and Micah McCreary assert that it is an established fact that African Americans look to their church or pastor in times of crisis (illness, family matters, mental health issues).[54] Thus, Black pastors and those in leadership in Black churches need to be informed about mental health issues, especially the many variations of depression. When pastors and leaders in Black churches learn how to identify, assess, and provide aid to those women who may need it, depression becomes less of an unknown challenge that impedes human flourishing.

Second, Black churches need to be actively engaged in partnerships with community agencies that provide mental health services and be ready to make referrals. Kim Stansbury and her coauthors contend that clergy in Black churches are often viewed by their constituents to be readily accessible persons whom they can speak to about their social and emotional problems.[55] Because of this, they see clergy as contacts who can connect persons who suffer from depression or mental health problems with appropriate mental health services. Stansbury et al assert, "A majority of individuals seek assistance from clergy exclusively and do not seek additional care from physicians or specialty mental health personnel. This frontline vantage point places African American clergy in an important position to act as gatekeepers to the formal mental health system."[56] Howard Clinebell and Margaret McKeever suggest that clergy should go beyond an informal knowing to having established relationships with mental health professionals and mental health agencies in which they can serve as a bridge connecting the person with the mental health professional or agency who is known personally and trusted.[57]

Third, Black churches must expand, embrace, and support the reality of the various ways in which Black families are constituted within their congregations. Discussing single-parent households, James Perkins writes, "When husbands and wives divorce, when unmarried women have children, when married women have children and become widowed, when married women have children and are divorced or are deserted by their husbands, or when wives die or desert their husbands, the end result is the same: single-parent households."[58] According to the statistics on African American women, 29% of all African American households are headed by single Black women.[59] Many of these women attend Black churches along with their children and look to the church to provide them with spiritual and emotional support as they deal with the exigencies of life particular to their single status. The continued celebration of the nuclear family as the ego-ideal within Black churches can be oppressive, particularly because the majority of families in Black churches are outside of the norm of this dominant Eurocentric model. Nancy Boyd-Franklin asserts that just because a household is headed by a single female does not necessarily mean it is dysfunctional. She writes, "Many African American single parents who have never been married function well as parents, and their children grow up to be capable adults. Many divorced or separated Black single parents . . . are functional as well."[60] Johnny Hill contends,

> The black family has never been prototypical model based on Eurocentric standards. Since slavery, the black family has taken on many forms. More often than not,

> the black family has been characterized by relationships built on trust and interdependency and not necessarily on the commonly idealistic nuclear family unit of two heterosexual parents with children.[61]

While the nuclear family may serve as the model to aspire to due to the advantages that it offers, such as two sources of -income and shared care of children, it can no longer be the only family constellation celebrated within the life of the congregation. Single-parent families, especially those headed by women, need to be embraced and supported as well. Leadership in Black churches should assess the needs of its single-parent households and be prepared to develop viable ministries and programs of support to alleviate some of the stressors that often confront these families (caring for children, sole provider for the household, poverty, etc.) and that might predispose single African American women to dysthymia. These initiatives may include affordable childcare, afterschool tutorial programs, afterschool care for latchkey kids whose parents are working, advocacy for a living wage, and access to culturally conscious and affordable counseling.

Fourth, in addition to already existent singles support groups, Black churches would do well to create therapeutic support groups for African American single women where they can find an outlet to explore and express their feelings and thoughts about what it means to be African American, female, and single in today's world. These therapeutic support groups would serve as a safe space for single Black women who share a particular desire for marriage that continues to be unfulfilled. Due to the nature of issues that having children presents, there would need to be two groups: one for singles without children and another for single parents with children. Unlike the existent singles ministry groups, these therapeutic support groups would be more developed and structured to address issues for single women who may be more predisposed to dysthymia. The aim of these groups would be to provide women with the opportunity for self-exploration and self-awareness on issues such as the desire for marriage, loneliness, depression, learning to take care of oneself emotionally and physically, and envisioning one's life in the future. Facilitated by women who are skilled in mental health issues, these groups, when constructed as small and intimate (i.e., closed with participation kept at small numbers), can provide a greater opportunity for self-revelation and healing. These therapeutic groups would need to run at least one year and offer pre-, post-, and midyear evaluations to assess their effectiveness in treating core issues relative to African American single women who desire marriage but for whom this desire remains ever elusive.

Fifth, Black churches must focus their attention on the self-development of African American males, many of whom are raised by single females where a male figure is absent in the household. In general, some Black churches already implement boys' rites of passage and mentoring programs that seek to provide moral and spiritual guidance very early in the developmental life cycle of the African American male youth. While these initiatives are well and good, they are not enough. There needs to be intentionality in this area, especially in regard to healthy relationships and healthy marriages. Robert Franklin identifies healthy relationships as ". . . interpersonal bonds and interactions that are characterized by mutuality, trust, respect, nonviolence, and sharing."[62] In this respect, there must be greater emphasis on mentoring Black males by Black men who are committed to providing a stable nurturing relationship and example. In this context, lifespan themes like identity, education, employment, careers, healthy dating, marriage, family life, and sexuality must be part of the curriculum. The purpose of these programs is to be deliberate in cultivating African American males who would potentially become eligible suitors and marriage partners for those African American single women who may desire marriage. This is especially important since many African American single women in Black churches subscribe to the traditional view that "he who finds a wife finds a good thing and obtains favor from the Lord" (Proverbs 18:22). Given this reality, training programs that emphasize marriage as a positive value for African American males is vital. Franklin affirms that the best people to instill and promote the institution of marriage among Black males are those Black men who are actively engaged in secure and happy marriages.[63]

Last, Black churches must engage in the work of social justice advocacy that seeks to address the societal ills perpetuated by structures of oppression—racism, classism, sexism—that impact the quality of lives of single African American women. Mass incarceration, unemployment, substandard education, substance abuse, homicide, and violence create an undue burden for African Americans in general and compound the singleness of African American females in particular. In addition, it also reduces the pool of potential suitors for African American women.[64] The gender oppression prevalent in many Black churches attacks women's sense of self. Poverty only serves to compound women's sense of hopelessness as they seek human fulfillment in America. Black churches' involvement in speaking out on these social issues could serve to convey to single African American women that they are not alone in their struggle with depression and or singleness, and that the Black institution to which they look to for spiritual support partners with them in their attempts to be fully human and reap the rewards that full participation in American society brings.

Conclusion

Undertaking some or all of the pastoral care initiatives mentioned above are hopeful avenues that Black churches can pursue to support African American women whose desire for marriage remains unrealized and whose depression might exacerbated by being single. Moreover, while some churches offer various supportive ministries for their congregants (marriage, single, youth), others have yet to provide similar support for their single members. Where these churches give prominence to their married constituency, a more intentional effort must be made to include ministries that provide space for non-married members to have healthy dialogues about concerns that affect and impact them directly. We acknowledge that what healing looks like in this context is challenging given that each woman's assessment of her singleness and its connection to her depression is unique. In other words, healing in this context is deeply personal and involves a journey of self-discovery, acceptance, and adjustment. Nevertheless, we suggest that a strong network of friends and family (inside and outside the church) is often vital for helping women make the first moves in this regard.

The Leah dynamic as it relates to choice or preference of a marriage partner may resonate with the experience of some Black women whose desire to be "preferred" as a marriage partner remains unrealized. This absence may trigger feelings of self-loathing and despair. Addressing this dilemma necessitates focusing both on the plight of single Black women as well as on making Black men more accessible suitors for single Black women. The pervasiveness of depression, specifically among African American women in Black churches, compels the creation of ministries explicitly designed to educate and promote mental health awareness, wholeness, and healing. Implementing pastoral care initiatives within the congregation to address the concerns of those suffering from depression, while challenging, can have a tremendous impact by providing much needed support through counseling and referrals to licensed professionals. In essence, pastoral care initiatives around depression can be life affirming, and thus lifesaving, as the "Leahs" in our congregations may tell us once the silence (and suffering) has been broken.

Discussion Questions

- When understood in the context of depression, how can Leah's experience aid Black women in fostering empathetic and supportive relationships?

- Given the biblical portrait of Leah's struggle with depression and that it is a reality for some (not all) Black women, to what extent should Black churches engage in caring for the mental and emotional well-being of their congregants?

- In what way(s) does the mental and emotional well-being of congregants of Black churches intersect matters of justice as it relates to people of color?

- What specific ministry strategies can Black churches develop that address the mental and emotional well-being of female congregants as it relates to the issue of depression?

Additional Resources

Jessica Young Brown, *Making SPACE at the Well: Mental Health and the Church* (Judson Press, 2020).

Rabbi Shai Held and Rabbi Yitz Greenberg, "Can We Be Grateful and Disappointed at the Same Time?: Or, What Leah Learned," in *The Heart of Torah*, volume 1, *Essays on the Weekly Torah Portion: Genesis and Exodus* (University of Nebraska Press, 2017), 60–63.

Pamela Robinson, *The Color of HOPE: African American Mental Health in the Church* (Fortitude Graphic Design & Printing, 2020).

Howard Stone, *Defeating Depression: Real Help for You and Those Who Love You*, 2nd edition (CreateSpace Publishing Platform, 2014).

Endnotes

1 Rachel Havrelock, "Genesis 28:10–32:3: The Journey Within," in *The Torah: A Women's Commentary* (URJ Press, 2008), 157.

2 Amy Kalmanofsky, *Dangerous Sisters of the Hebrew Bible* (Fortress Press, 2014), 22.

3 Morton Seelenfreund and Stanley Schneider, "Leah's Eyes," *Jewish Bible Quarterly* 25, no. 1 (1997): 19–20.

4 L. Daniel Hawk, "Cast Out and Cast Off," *Priscilla Papers Old Testament* 25, no. 1 (2011): 11.

5 Seelenfreund and Schneider, "Leah's Eyes," 20.

6 Biblical references to the eye or eyes appear over five hundred times and suggest the significance of this optical organ to ancient Israelite concepts of justice, ethics, and morality (see Exodus 21:24; Deuteronomy 32:10; Judges 18:6; and Psalm 17:8).

7 *Diagnostic and Statistical Manual of Mental Disorders: DSM-5* (American Psychiatric Publishing, 2013).

8 Sigmund Freud, "Mourning and Melancholia," *Collected Papers*, vol. IV (Hogarth, 1917), 155.

9 Ibid., 153–55.

10 Ibid., 155–58.

11 Ibid., 153.

12 Ibid., 153.

13 Susan J. Dunlap, *Counseling Depressed Women* (Westminster John Knox Press, 1997), 22.

14 Ibid.

15 Ibid.

16 Ibid.

17 Christie Cozad Neuger, *Counseling Women: A Narrative, Pastoral Approach* (Fortress Press, 2001), 152.

18 Ibid., 152.

19 Ronald W. Richardson, *Creating a Healthier Church: Family Systems Theory, Leadership, and Congregational Life* (Fortress Press, 1996), 144.

20 Ibid., 144.

21 Ibid., 149–50.

22 For an interesting interpretation of the sibling rivalry between Leah and Rachel, see Carolyn B. Helsel and Song-Mi Suzie Park's article, "The Traps of Competitive Parenting: Keeping Up with Rachel and Leah," in *The Flawed Family of God: Stories About the Imperfect Families in Genesis* (Westminster John Knox, 2021), 101–14. However, as Kalmanofsky points out in reference to the mandrake episode, the two sisters "compromise and cooperate to get what they want." See Kalmanofsky, *Dangerous Sisters of the Hebrew Bible*, 28.

23 Renita J. Weems, *Just a Sister Away: Understanding the Timeless Connection Between Women of Today and Women in the Bible* (Walk Worthy Press, 2005), 61.

24 According to Helsel and Park, Laban's actions place Leah in a very peculiar situation in which she is caught up in a loveless marriage to a man who never wanted to marry her in the first place. See Helsel and Park, "The Traps of Competitive Parenting," 104.
25 Helsel and Park, "The Traps of Competitive Parenting," 103–4.
26 Freud, "Mourning and Melancholia," 159.
27 Ibid., 155–6; Dunlap, *Counseling Depressed Women*, 22.
28 Neuger, *Counseling Women*, 150.
29 Edward J. Bridge, "A Mother's Influence: Mothers Naming Children in the Hebrew Bible," *Vetus Testamentum* 64, no. 3 (2014): 392.
30 Wilma Bailey, "Intimate Moments: A Study of Genesis 29:31–30:21," *Proceedings* 29 (2009): 5.
31 Joan Ross-Burstall, "Leah and Rachel: A Tale of Two Sisters," *Word & World* 14, no. 2 (1994): 168.
32 Hawk, "Cast Out and Cast Off," 11.
33 Here I am drawing upon the work of J. William Worden, *Grief Counseling and Grief Therapy*, who identifies four tasks of mourning: accept the reality of the loss; process the pain of grief; adjust to a world without the deceased; and find an enduring connection with the deceased while embarking on a new life.
34 Terrance Fretheim, "The Book of Genesis: Introduction, Commentary, and Reflections," in *New Interpreter's Bible Volume I: General & Old Testament Articles, Genesis, Exodus, Leviticus* (Abingdon Press, 1994), 554.
35 Myrna M. Weissman and Gerald L. Klerman, "Sex Differences and the Epidemiology of Depression," *Archives of General Psychiatry* 34, no. 1 (1977): 98–111, https://doi.org/10.1001/archpsyc.1977.01770130100011; Dunlap, *Counseling Depressed Women*, 2–3; Howard Stone, *Depression and Hope: New Insights for Pastoral Counseling* (Fortress Press, 1998), 42–44; Susan Nolen-Hoeksema, *Sex Differences in Depression* (Stanford University Press, 1990), 21–76.
36 Neuger, *Counseling Women*, 150.
37 Stone, *Depression and Hope*, 11.
38 Neuger, *Counseling Women*, 160.
39 Chanequa Walker-Barnes, *Too Heavy a Yoke: Black Women and the Burden of Strength* (Cascade Books, 2014), 54.
40 Walker-Barnes, *Too Heavy a Yoke*, 55.

41 John T. Cacioppo et al., "Loneliness as a Specific Risk Factor for Depressive Symptoms: Cross-Sectional and Longitudinal Analyses," *Psychology & Aging* 21, no. 1 (2006): 148.

42 See "Black Marriage in America," *Black Demographics*.

43 Ibid.

44 On Black women's loyalty to marrying within the race, see "Black Marriage in America."

45 We acknowledge the fact that not all single Black women desire marriage.

46 Walker-Barnes, *Too Heavy a Yoke*, 22.

47 Ibid., 23.

48 "Black Marriage in America," *Black Demographics*.

49 *The Diagnostic and Statistical Manual of Mental Disorders*, 5th ed., 168–71. "Criteria for Persistent Depressive Disorder (Dysthymia): Depressed mood for most of the day for at least two years, presence of two or more symptoms while depressed, poor appetite or overeating, insomnia or hypersomnia, low energy/fatigue, low self-esteem, poor concentration, feelings of hopelessness. Major depressive disorder may precede persistent depressive disorder or may occur simultaneously with PDD. People can be dually diagnosed with MDD and PDD. Dysthymia is differentiated from Major Depressive Disorder by length of the depression (no less than two years in duration) and fewer symptoms (person must exhibit at least three symptoms)."

50 Terrie Williams, *Black Pain: It Just Looks Like We're Not Hurting* (Scribner, 2008), 1.

51 Walker-Barnes, *Too Heavy a Yoke*, 36.

52 Anahvia Taiyib Mewborn, "Recognizing Cultural Dysthymia: The Implications of Including Discrimination Mediated Mental Illnesses in the Diagnostic and Statistical Manual of Mental Disorders," *Journal of Undergraduate Research and Scholarly Excellence* 6 (2015): 42–45.

53 Mewborn, "Recognizing Cultural Dysthymia," 42–45.

54 Jessica Young Brown and Micah L. McCreary, "Pastoral Counseling Practices and Perceptions of Mental Health Services: Implications for African American Mental Health," *Journal of Pastoral Care & Counseling* 68 (2014): 1–14. See also Chapter 7 of Nancy Boyd Franklin, *Black Families in Therapy* on how Black churches prominently impact the lives of African Americans.

55 Kim L. Stansbury et al., "African American Clergy: What Are Their Perceptions of Pastoral Care and Pastoral Counseling?," *Journal of Religious Health* 51 (2012): 961–69.

56 Stansbury et al., "African American Clergy," 962.

57 Howard Clinebell, *Basic Types of Pastoral Care and Counseling: Resources for the Ministry of Healing and Growth*, ed. Bridget Clare McKeever (Abingdon Press, 2011), 404.

58 James C. Perkins, *Building Up Zion's Walls: Ministry for Empowering the African American Family* (Judson Press, 1999), 89.

59 "Black Women Statistics," *Black Demographics*, https://blackdemographics.com/population/black-women-statistics/.

60 Nancy Boyd-Franklin, *Black Families in Therapy: Understanding the African American Experience* (The Guilford Press, 2006), 287.

61 Johnny Hill, *Multidimensional Ministry for Today's Black Family* (Judson Press, 2007), 3.

62 Robert Franklin, *Crisis in the Village: Restoring Hope in African American Communities* (Fortress Press, 2007), 53.

63 Franklin, Crisis in the Village, 70–72.

64 For a thorough analysis of mass incarceration, see Michelle Alexander, *The New Jim Crow: Mass Incarceration in the Age of Colorblindness* (The New Press, 2010). On developing ministries to persons and families affected by mass incarceration, see W. Wilson Goode Sr. et al., eds., *Ministry with Prisoners & Families: The Way Forward* (Judson Press, 2011). On unemployment, see William Julius Wilson, *The Truly Disadvantaged: The Inner City, the Underclass, and Public Policy*, 2nd ed. (Chicago University Press, 2012).

2

Grief and Melancholia among African Immigrants in the United States: Insights for Pastoral Care and Counseling, Genesis 11–25

M. Fulgence Nyengele

This chapter will explore the losses and grief associated with the immigration experience of Africans in the United States. Relevant chapters in the biblical immigration story of Abraham and Sarah in Genesis 11–25 will be read together with the experience of African immigrants to highlight some major issues immigrants typically encounter. While immigration generally involves excitement in pursuing a new life and new opportunities, this experience also includes the invisible, yet powerful pain of loss involved in relocating to a new environment. African immigrants, like all immigrants, face several challenges even as they achieve successes in their new home.

The experience of immigration entails various forms of loss including loss of homeland, language, culture, status, religious practices, community, and social environment, among others. And the feelings of loss can last for several years. Understanding the grief experience associated with immigration as a natural and necessary part of migratory loss and, therefore, of immigrants' lives, could enable churches and pastors to build empathic communities that attend to the acculturative struggles and cultural mourning of (African) immigrants by developing strategies for responding to the spiritual and emotional needs associated with the challenges of living through migratory loss. With empathic pastoral support, migratory grief and cultural melancholia can be transformed into creativity and hope.

The Immigration Experience of Africans

"The United States is becoming an increasingly attractive destination for African immigrants, with their numbers more than doubling since 2000. Although some are coming from war-torn countries, the immigrants also include large numbers of highly educated professionals . . . doctors, engineers and others immigrating to the country in search of a better life."[1] In his account about his personal experience as an African-born immigrant trying to find professional work in the United States and create a sense of home, Lombe M. Mwembo, a professional educator and scholar of education with a PhD from an American university, describes the struggles and challenges of trying to find a dream job that matched his qualifications and professional experience.[2] His journey and struggle begin in his native Democratic Republic of Congo, where he had returned after receiving his master's degree in education in the United States. Despite his effort, he could not find a position that corresponded with his education and training.

Mwembo writes about his professional experience prior to going to the Unites States for further education as a springboard for telling his story of struggle when he immigrated to the United States. He had worked in a prominent role at World Vision, an international nonprofit organization, and served as principal of a prestigious school in his native Congo. But returning to the Congo after gaining his master's degree proved very frustrating as he was not able to find a good paying job that corresponded with his level of education and expertise. He attributes this to the country being at war and job opportunities being limited because of the social and economic instability caused by war.[3] He therefore decided to go back to the United States in the hope that he would get such a job, save some money, and at some point return to his homeland to become his own boss, running his own business.[4] He also dreamed about getting a doctorate to increase his chances of becoming more marketable. But what he experienced in the United Sates when he returned was very disappointing. He did not anticipate that he would encounter significant challenges of not only adjusting to the culture, but also the struggles of getting a good paying job as a "skilled" immigrant. Mwembo writes:

I could not have imagined the challenges I would go through when I returned to the United States to look for work. I had to find a place to stay and make money to pay rent and utility bills. I did not imagine that it would take several months to adjust my immigration status, apply for employment authorization, and wait there without an income. Least of all did I imagine that the color of my skin and my place of origin would get in the way of my obtaining employment. Six months went by, and I still lacked a good source of income. I was compelled to take some strange jobs that no one with my level of education would ever consider. I went from being a school principal at one of the prestigious Belgian schools in the Congo and a manager at World Vision International to working on campus as a security guard. I was frustrated, confused, and disillusioned. In Africa, I used to be respected by adults and students and held in high esteem by the community. Now, in America, I was losing all the respect and honor because of my race and nationality.[5]

Mwembo goes on to discuss how humbling it was to accept the position as a security guard and the pain of feeling diminished by this experience.[6] He recounts how his weekly pay was the equivalent of one-tenth of his pay in the DRC before he left for graduate studies in the United States. He was not able to support himself on that small pay and was embarrassingly unable to send any money to support his wife and children whom he left in the Congo awaiting to be invited to join him when he would get a good job. Like many immigrants in his immigrant community, he kept on hoping and praying for a better tomorrow. Some of his African friends encouraged him to persevere, and he was inspired by a saying that many shared with him: "No pain, no gain." Although he was resilient and endured the pain that characterized his initial immigration experience, his story captures the ongoing and pervasive struggles and challenges many immigrants of color—and especially African immigrants—face.[7]

Later, Mwembo found jobs that corresponded with his level of education and professional experience. But these did not preclude him from encountering even more daunting challenges due to unwelcoming attitudes, prejudices, and racism. In his work as a therapeutic support person, a teacher in private and public school systems, and as an adjunct college professor, he encountered significant obstacles due to prejudices towards his race and national origin. Noting the prevalent ignorance about Africa and Africans that he found in American schools, Mwembo tells stories about how some children loved to call him African (as if it was a negative thing) and to follow that up with statements such as "Africans smell; Africa is a jungle" and "You people in Africa, do you sleep with animals and snakes in the trees?" These encounters and interactions were particularly painful because "to be asked those questions by little children [or teenagers] was the most humiliating experience for me as an educator."[8] This is something he could never even imagine happening in the Congo where he had worked as a teacher, school principal, and manager of a nonprofit organization. He was viewed as an elder, and to be an elder commanded respect and admiration from the community—including children, parents, colleagues, and others. Indeed, adding insult to injury was the prevalent negative perception of his English accent. He recalls once entering a classroom and hearing his students say: "Mr. Mwembo does not know how to speak English." On another occasion when he was applying for a teaching job, the school principal said straightforwardly, "He is good and has an outstanding resume, but my students' parents will not accept someone who speaks English with an accent to teach their children." His disappointment was even deeper because he questioned how Christian parents and a Christian principal of a Christian school could openly discriminate against another Christian based on the way that other Christian (or non-Christian for that matter) speaks English with an African accent.[9] In his 2009 doctoral dissertation, Dr. Mwembo wrote about how most of what the American public and American teachers know about Congolese and African immigrants is based solely on biased media coverage, biased old stories, and myths that are not supported by valid research.[10] He states:

> As a result of the lack of research about African immigrants and their children, not only have the special needs of these immigrants been neglected, but Congolese [and other African] students in American schools continue to be victims of demeaning treatments and attacks, including violent attacks by some American students motivated by ignorance, prejudice, misconceptions and stereotypes.[11]

I have discussed Dr. Mwembo's story at some length to show how difficult the immigration experience of African immigrants is and especially how racism and linguicism complicate their adjustment process, making a bad situation even worse. Dr. Mwembo's chapter is part of an edited book of fourteen chapters by African-born immigrant educators and academics living in the United States.[12] His lived experience is corroborated by many of these authors as they share their own experience and immigration journeys.

The book discusses the immigration experience of African immigrants coming from various African countries, including Burundi, Cameroon, Democratic Republic of Congo, Ghana,

Nigeria, Senegal, South Africa, and Zimbabwe. It explores the challenges and existential realities confronting these immigrants in the United States, their complex assimilation or adaptation processes as teachers, students, and parents, including the employment difficulties they are facing, the problems related to how their English accent is perceived, and cultural conflicts, among other things. The similarities of their lived experiences as immigrants are staggering.[13]

Omiunota N. Ukpokodu, who contributed the foreword to the book, affirms that "African-born educators and immigrant students, regardless of credentials, competence, or productivity, are relegated to the background and treated as the 'other.' Being Black, African and accented—biological conditions that are beyond one's control—are used to dehumanize and disenfranchise them."[14] Recognizing the similarity between her experiences of marginalization and disrespect and those of some contributors to this book, Ukpokodu writes:

> My first exposure to the American college classroom was a total shock—student disrespect toward me as the professor, lack of classroom civility and disregard for the teaching/learning process—nothing I had ever seen. I came from a culture and educational institutions where there was high regard, reverence for and deference to the teacher or professor. In college in Nigeria, students respectfully addressed and called professors/instructors "Prof." Respect was a given regardless of the cultural, social, intellectual and linguistic characteristics of the teacher/professor, unless the person had engaged in disgraceful or shameful behavior. But I found that in most American classrooms, respect is conditional—depending on the cultural, racial, ethnic and linguistic similarity.[15]

In keeping with the theme of experiencing shock at the disrespect she has experienced as an immigrant college professor, Ukpokodu tells the story of being shocked even more deeply when a student stood up during one of her classes and asked a disrespectful and racist question: "I want to know why people from Africa are coming here to teach us when they are not Americans!" Even though several students booed this student and told him to sit down, Ukpodoku says that she was still profoundly shocked at this student's audacity and disrespect, and says that she was not prepared for the overt and covert racism and ethnocentrism of the students—although she recognizes that not all the American students she encountered were disrespectful or rude.[16] But the pain and suffering caused by these interactions are real: "These experiences are deeply painful and often create a feeling of the 'outsider' and the perpetual stranger, which contribute to job dissatisfaction and the dilemma of whether to remain in self-exile or return to one's homeland for good."[17] Again, this speaks to the complex immigration experience of African immigrants in the United States.

Zimbabwean Francis Musoni and his colleagues have also published a very informative book based on oral history interviews with forty-seven African-born immigrants living in Kentucky.[18] Suggesting that every African-born person they interviewed for their book has a unique and complex story, the authors nevertheless name challenges and issues similar to those observed by Dr. Mwembo and his colleagues, in the book edited by Immaculée Harushimana and her colleagues. Musoni and his colleagues mention the following challenges and issues as characterizing the immigration and assimilation process of African-born immigrants living in Kentucky: language, loneliness, cultural differences, issues related to credentials for employment, ignorance towards Africa, and racism. The Kentucky group also noted some positive experiences such as education, job opportunities, and helpful people.[19]

While many African immigrants acknowledge that immigration can bring new joys and opportunities to better their lives, including celebrating their professional achievements, they also recognize that starting a new life as an immigrant is not easy for immigrants of color.[20] Moving from their country of origin to a new country can be stressful and mentally and emotionally demanding. Studies show that "many immigrants from Asia, Latin America, the Caribbean, and Africa encounter racial discrimination for the first time in the United States, which can have a substantial impact on their health and mental health."[21] This is why the losses and grief involved in the immigration process must be acknowledged. And recognizing migratory grief is an important dimension of adjusting and adapting to the new environment. Before discussing the nature of the grief experienced in migration and the cultural melancholia related to these losses, perhaps a word on the persistence and determination of African immigrants is in order.

Nonye C. Obiora, who is originally from Nigeria, reinforces the need to confront the barriers set by prejudices, racism, and low expectations African immigrants encounter as students, educators, and parents. Decrying the invisibility and discrimination against African immigrants in the United States, Obiora encourages the quest for excellence and determination to pursue the dreams that brought African-born immigrants to these shores in the first place. Rather than be discouraged by the multiple enduring or entrenched obstacles he personally encountered, he saw them as "a catalyst for accelerating his career to the level he has achieved."[22] He talks about how his hard work and high motivation paid off when he was selected by the school district to become a teacher-leader in 2006, after overcoming significant barriers. This opportunity opened even more doors for him as he ended up being invited to participate in a national study on teaching mathematics. He writes: "It is hard to describe what it felt like to stand in front of a classroom consisting of 97% Caucasian educators, facilitating a mathematics seminar with my *funny* accent. It wouldn't have been possible if I had given in to the pressure of my otherness and thrown in the towel."[23] Obiora goes on to say that he is sharing his story in order to inspire African-born teachers and other foreign-born teachers of color to be courageous, determined, and confident that they can succeed, if they continue to affirm themselves and work hard. He concludes that "non-white immigrant teachers can be *foreign*, or speak with a *funny* accent; however, through perseverance and excellence, we have been able to demonstrate that we are not *inferior*."[24] Indeed, many African-born immigrants have the capacity to shape a new life for themselves in their new home away from home. This sense of strength and resilience has been observed among many first-generation immigrants of various backgrounds in the United States.[25]

However, not everybody is successful or lucky. While most African immigrants are citizens, or they have legal status as permanent residents, or are in the country with work or family visas or refugee status, a good number of African immigrants are also in limbo.[26] Reasons for this state are unique to each person's mode of entry, as refugee fleeing political violence and war or immigrant in search for work, education, and a better life, who for some reason have not been able to secure legal status and find a good paying job. As Teresa Wiltz writes, "Immigration experts say that black immigrants face more discrimination and scrutiny than other migrant groups. Many of the challenges they face intersect with the challenges of native-born African-Americans, from housing discrimination to disproportionate representation in the criminal justice system."[27] This is the case because in most instances, communities where most black immigrants live are heavily policed. This makes them vulnerable in many ways because local policing and practices push many black immigrants into the criminal justice system for minor offenses, which may cause deportation proceedings and make it really difficult to fight deportation. But many are working hard to assimilate into the culture and become productive members of society. This is why the creation of advocacy boards is one of the central concerns in many black immigrant communities. More recently, for example, Ohio's African immigrants celebrated the long-awaited approval of the New African Immigrants Commission, which advocates for the needs of sub-Saharan African immigrants and refugees living in Ohio. The commission was created in 2008, but it took almost ten years to get the group finally approved in 2017 and the eleven-member board appointed.[28]

The commission names the following challenges facing the African immigrants in the State of Ohio: integrating into American culture; becoming self-sufficient; learning English; getting access to education and health care; connecting with transportation; accessing legal services and other needed resources. The commission also intends to show its accomplishments. For example, the commission reported that forty-one percent of the state's foreign-born black population has higher-education degrees, compared with twenty-eight percent of the general US population.[29] The commission began its work in 2018 and hopes to host seminars, events, and workshops that address the needs and issues of the community.

Gender and the Immigration of Experience of African Women

Before exploring the story of Abraham and Sarah, a word on gender differences in the immigration experiences of African men and women is in order. In her study of African women immigrants living in Minnesota, Njeri M. Clement observes that to be black African and a woman in a world in which powerful patriarchal and racial forces construe both these identities as inferior is an important factor in understanding gender in African women's immigration experience.[30] This means that in addition to encountering racism, African women also encounter sexism and gender-based prejudice. While sexism is not necessarily a new experience for African women, given the fact that they most likely had encountered it in African cultures before immigrating to the United States,[31] the intersecting experience of racism, sexism, and gender-based prejudice further complicates women's lives and the process of negotiating their adaptation and assimilation in their new land.

For example, the disrespect and "lack of civility and disregard" that Omiunota Ukpokodu encountered in her teaching could be attributed to the convergence not only of racism and the ethnocentrism of her students as she indicates, but also sexism—even though she does not explicitly include sexism as a factor in the way the students disrespectfully related to her in the classroom.

It is important to be mindful of assimilation differences between women and men immigrants because gender-based violence is endemic to women's experience of migration. Research shows that even though nearly half of migrants worldwide are women, "scholarly literature on migrants rarely discuss women's gendered experiences of migration."[32] Women immigrants are more likely to experience sexual violence in its various manifestations: rape, sexual torture, being forced to exchange sex for protection, sexual harassment, and sexual exploitation, among many others.[33] Indeed, immigration must be understood from a gendered lens because men and women inhabit different gendered spaces in society and because gender is overtly or covertly linked to the cultural values, ideologies, and power relations involved in the assimilation and acculturation processes.[34]

Clement argues that "African women immigrants' gender identities take [multiple] dimensions, including 'Black,' immigrants, third world, or 'other,' all of which obscure and complicate their sense of 'selves' and compound the efforts to make sense of who they are in their 'home away from home.'"[35] She goes on to suggest that being positioned within the intersection of race, class, gender, and nationality creates particular vulnerabilities that African women immigrants have to deal with in the assimilation and acculturation processes. However, it is important to note that while the immigration process presents significant barriers and difficulties based on gender, migrating to the United States does also provide opportunities to improve women's social or gender-related status, leading to improved social status and professional development. The African women immigrants that Clement interviewed did not only discuss the gender-based challenges and difficulties they encountered, but also proudly highlighted their educational and professional achievements and the contributions they are making to their "home away from home."[36] Another study of African women immigrants living in the Greater Boston area and Philadelphia also corroborates the findings of Clement's study on ways in which the intersections of gender, race, class, and nationality affect women's immigration to the United States and the ways they make sense of their lives and overcome the barriers they encounter in the assimilation process, and how all these efforts lead African women immigrants to make significant contributions to society.[37]

The Story of Abraham and Sarah

> Now the Lord said to Abram, "Go from your country and your kindred and your father's house to the land that I will show you." (Genesis 12:1)[38]

Most people in the church read the story of Abraham as a story of faith and obedience to God. Abraham is viewed as an exemplar of faith and obedience to God's call to go where God sent him. While this reading reflects the spiritual and theological aspects of Abraham's life and vocation, and even the Bible itself supports this reading,[39] it seems to overlook the existential push and pull of migration that also contributed to Abraham's migratory lifestyle. Seeing Abraham primarily as a progenitor of a faith and as a patriarch, and not as a migrant, fails to recognize the real-life existential challenges and circumstances that might have also forced him to migrate.Abraham and Sarah moved by necessity—and, in some respects, by force—because of difficult circumstances.

Zorodzai Dube, a South African biblical scholar, critiques the typical reading of the story of Abraham as a story of faith and obedience to God's calling and a lesson on how to faithfully listen to God's voice, despite all odds.[40] Dube argues that this focus prevents us from seeing the profound human quest for stability and comfort that propelled Abraham to migrate.[41] He goes on to say that, "Abraham was primarily a nomad . . . meaning that he migrated from one geographical location to the other in search of pasture and food." Dube goes on to add that "food and sustenance are the primary questions to migrants—[and that] these [must] be seen as pull or push factors [in the life of Abraham]."[42]

The story of Abraham and Sarah's migration begins in Genesis 11:27–32 when Terah, father of Abraham, took his family or clan from Ur of the Chaldeans to go to the land of Canaan, "but when they came to Haran, they settled there" (Genesis 11:31). There is no explanation about why Terah chose to go to Canaan, although it seems like "Canaan would be a not unattractive destination," as Keith N. Grüneberg suggests.[43] Neither is there any reason given why Terah and his family left Ur of the Chaldeans, or why they decided to remain in Haran. In Genesis 11:27–28, we are told that Terah had three sons: Abram, Nahor, and Haran. We are also told that Haran was the father of Lot whom Terah took with him when he set out to go to the land of Canaan. The text states that Haran, Lot's father, died in Ur of the Chaldeans, his land of birth. Abram was married to Sarai and Nahor was married to Milcah, the daughter of Haran who died in Ur of the Chaldeans (Genesis 11:29). Again, it is worth noting that, even though the text does not say why Terah took his family out of Ur of the Chaldeans to go to the land of Canaan, it is curious that the death of Haran in Ur of the Chaldeans is mentioned. Moreover, it is intriguing that Terah took his "grandson Lot son of Haran" to be a part of the family and group that went with him to Haran. Could the apparent early death of Haran have caused Terah and his family to leave Ur of the Chaldeans? What were the circumstances of Haran's death? Although the text is silent on all this, we can only ask questions and wonder if this presumably premature death and loss of a son who died *before* his father Terah (Genesis 11:28) was a factor in Terah's decision to move and go to another place. We can also only wonder if including Lot as a part of the group that was moving with the family might also signal some intent to protect him from a possible similar fate like his father, and to give him opportunities to grow and continue his father Haran's name? The text states that Terah died in Haran at 205 years of age (Genesis 11:32), and Abraham decided to leave Haran after his father had died. Did Terah's death and the related undisclosed difficulties cause Abraham to move, and to take with him his nephew Lot, in order to protect him like his father Terah did?

This context is important because when God calls Abraham, he tells him to go from his country, his kindred, and his father's house to go to the land that God will show him (Genesis 12:1). In a real sense, Abraham had already left his native land of Ur of the Chaldeans at his father's injunction, for reasons that are not explained. And he was already in some way on the way toward the land of Canaan with his father before receiving the personal call to leave. Now he has to leave the new place (Haran) and his relatives (again) and everything that was familiar to him and to Sarah to go to the land of Canaan because, with his father's death, "there is nothing to hold him in Haran,"[44] as there probably is nothing left in his father's house.

Genesis 12:1 introduces Abraham's call as a story of migration: "Now the LORD said to Abram, 'Go from your country and your kindred and your father's house to the land I will show you.'" The language of "going from" or leaving the significant things he was connected to suggests that Abraham has to break the close ties with the place, the people, and the family or clan. This three-fold leave and the specific close ties he has to break "confirms the difficulty of what is asked [of Abraham]."[45] But the leave is "not only geographical in nature, but emotional and cultural as well."[46] The journey ahead will require significant efforts to adjust to the new place and the new realities he will have to face. Adding to the difficulty is the fact that Abraham does not know where he is going. Yet Genesis 12:2–9 is packed with promises and blessings, as if to acknowledge the difficulties and challenges involved in the three-fold act of leaving and to balance the demands of the command to go with the assurance of the promises and blessings. Grüneberg suggests that "the divine orders to travel despite the obvious risks involved in moving to a strange location are accompanied by assurance of divine favor."[47] As such this assurance is intended to convey a sense of security through the promises and blessings. From a psychological perspective, these promises and blessings can be viewed as an expression of Abraham's hope and dream for a better life and future. Thus, encouraged and sustained by the divine promises and blessings, "Abraham went, as the LORD told him; and Lot went with him" (Genesis 12:4). "Abraham took his wife Sarai and his brother's son Lot, and all the possessions that they had gathered, and the persons whom they had acquired in Haran; and they set forth to go to the land of Canaan" (Genesis 12:5).

It is interesting that Abraham and his people do not settle in the new land right away. He is moving from place to place probably to get to know well the land and possibly its inhabitants. The text says that "when they had come to the land of Canaan, Abram passed through the land to the place of Shechem, to the oak of Moreh," and we are told that "at that time the Canaanites were in the land" (Genesis 12:6). Grossman suggests that this statement reveals the silent conflict that is beginning to come to realization in the land of Canaan,[48] although there is no evidence at this point of any interactions between Abraham and the local inhabitants. God appears to Abraham and reinforces the promise that God will give this land to Abraham's offspring. (This promise is repeated in Genesis 15:18 when God makes a covenant with Abraham.) "So [Abraham] built there [i.e., at Shechem] an altar to the LORD, who had appeared to him" (Genesis 12:7), and he went on to Bethel, pitched his tent, built another altar to God, and then went on by stages toward the Negeb (Genesis 12:8-9). Abraham is literally a migrant who is moving from place to place to explore the land and establish altars and, in the process, getting himself familiarized with his new land—although he will always have the identity of a stranger, an alien residing among the Canaanites. Indeed, even later in his life, Abraham self-identified as "a stranger and an alien resident living among you" when he reached out to the Hittites to request that they sell to him the cave of Machpelah to bury his wife Sarah when she died (Genesis 23:3–6), a place where he will himself be buried in when he dies (Genesis 25:9–10). When Abimelech made a covenant with Abraham, he also referred to Abraham as someone who was residing in the land as *an alien* (Genesis 21:22–24). Lot, Abraham's nephew, is also referred to as *alien* in a disparaging way by the people of Sodom when he refused to comply with their demand that he brings out to them the two guests who were visiting: "And they said, 'This fellow [i.e., Lot] came here as an alien, and he would play the judge! Now we will deal worse with you than with them'" (Genesis 19:9).

However, it is important to note that Abraham was able to establish alliances and pleasant relationships with inhabitants of the land. As Grossman suggests, "Abram is not as lonely as one would think, since he forms alliances with the inhabitants of the land."[49] For example, when he returned from the battle in his efforts to find Lot and bring him back from captivity, the King of Sodom and King Melchizedek went out to greet him (Genesis 14:17–18). "And King Melchizedek of Salem brought out bread and wine; he was priest of God Most High. He blessed him and said: 'Blessed be Abram by God Most High, maker of heaven and earth; and blessed be God Most High, who has delivered your enemies into your hands!' And Abram gave him one tenth of everything" (Genesis 14:18–20). This interaction with Melchizedek and Abraham's response show some assimilation and accommodation to a dominant theological understanding and religious worldview from the dominant culture. Abraham here adopts the Canaanite view of *El Elyon* as "maker of heaven and earth."

At any rate, we can see that Abraham was a man on the move. He continued to travel through Canaan even after his return from Egypt. In Genesis 13, after returning from Egypt and regaining his Bethel location, Abraham is, for example, commanded "[to] rise up, walk through the length and the breadth of the land, for I will give it to you" (Genesis 13:17). Abraham settles only when he reaches the city of Hebron: "So Abraham moved his tent, and came and settled by the oaks of Mamre, which are at Hebron; and there he built an altar to the LORD" (Genesis 13:18). Only after Abraham had gone through his experiences in Egypt (Genesis 12) and separated from Lot (Genesis 13) does he truly settle in the land of Canaan.[50]

Going back to reasons why Abraham and Sarah were moving from one place to another, Genesis 12:10–20 provides a clear example of how existential threats forced Abraham and Sarah to migrate to Egypt: "Now there was a famine in the land. So Abram went down to Egypt to reside there as an alien, for the famine was severe in the land." The move to Egypt was clearly for survival reasons,. However, life in Egypt created other existential threats to both Abraham and Sarah, first as a couple, but also simply as people living as *alien* in a foreign land, forced to relocate by severe famine. In the effort to assimilate and adjust to the new situation, Abraham and Sarah are forced by circumstances to hide their true identity as a married couple. This is largely due to Abraham's worries and apparent anxiety about not only his personal safety, but his very survival. Therefore, he prepares Sarah prior to entering Egypt to lie that she was his sister. But Abraham was not completely off about his assumptions that when the Egyptians see Sarah, they would kill him if they knew that the two were a married couple. As soon as they entered Egypt, what Abraham anticipated happened. The Egyptians saw that Sarah was very beautiful and the officials praised her to Pharaoh, who took her into his house as his wife (Genesis 12:14–15). The text is silent about how Sarah dealt with this horrifying situation. But we can speculate. Sarah might have been horrified by this experience; she might have been shocked by the separation from her husband she had to endure, not to mention the sexual exploitation she had to suffer.

Gender differences clearly shape the migration experiences of Abraham and Sarah. Abraham is preoccupied with Sarah's appearance of beauty as an issue that may affect his own safety when they go to a new place. But this is all based on his perception and assumptions about the people he encounters in new places he travels to. Yet, as noted later in this chapter, Abraham's assumptions were not necessarily true in all circumstances. But the gender-based assimilation differences between Abraham and Sarah are evident. Indeed, while Abraham's life was safe, and Pharaoh dealt well with Abraham for Sarah's sake

(Genesis 12:16), Sarah's life was not only endangered, but she was also dehumanized. It feels as if Sarah had to be trafficked to ensure Abraham's survival and security. But God rescued Sarah by afflicting Pharaoh and his house with great plagues (Genesis 12:17), and Sarah returned to Abraham. However, Pharaoh ordered them to leave. Abraham and Sarah were forced to leave Egypt just as they were forcibly displaced from Canaan due to severe famine.

However, Abraham and Sarah remained vulnerable economic migrants who were still in quest for the land—for themselves; for their livestock; and for their offspring—all the divine promises and blessings notwithstanding. As noted earlier, when they returned from Egypt, they revisited the places they had lived in and ended up settling at the oaks of Mamre near Hebron. Then they went from there to Gerar where they resided *as aliens* (Genesis 20:1). But it is not clear what the motivation for traveling to Gerar is. As if the experience in Egypt was not instructive enough, Abraham *again* said that his wife Sarah was his sister. King Abimelech of Gerar "sent for and took Sarah" (Genesis 20:2). But God again rescued Sarah and she returned to Abraham. Unlike the situation in Egypt where they were forced to leave, here King Abimelech said to them, "My land is before you; settle where it pleases you" (Genesis 20:15), but not before engaging in a clarifying conversation with Abraham about his faulty assumptions with regard to what would happen to him if people in Gerar knew that Sarah was his wife (Genesis 20:9–20).

Megan Warner argues that "Abraham had been entirely wrong in his assessment of Gerar . . . Abraham's own fear that he would be killed on account of Sarah proves to be unfounded. Abraham is not harmed and in Genesis 20, as in each of the 'ancestress in danger' stories, the ancestor emerges from the events described heaped with material blessings."[51] Abraham's flawed assumptions could be indicative of acculturative stress, which refers to the specific reaction of immigrants in response to their adaptation and acculturation process and can be described as the "[stressful] changes following contact between culturally different people."[52]

So, we have in Abraham a picture of someone vulnerable and in need of the welcome and hospitality of the locals in Canaan (and Egypt) to sustain himself and his family in these socially and culturally stressful situations and "survive"—again, all the material wealth he acquired notwithstanding. David Carr writes the following about Abraham's situation:

> [Abraham] lives as a foreigner everywhere he goes—Canaan, Egypt, Philistia, on the Mediterranean coast—and finds himself vulnerable. But God protects and even enriches him while he lives in virtual exile. Like exiles, this biblical Abraham has doubts, repeatedly, about whether God will really follow through on God's promises of protection and blessing, asking, for example, "What will you give me, as I am now childless" (Genesis 17:17). He goes so far as to pass his wife off as his sister in order to protect himself in Egypt and Philistia, but God rescues him and his family anyway (12:10-20; 20:1–18).[53]

Joel Baden suggests that Abraham is the first immigrant—indeed, the first person who moved to live with people who were not his people. Once he and his people left Mesopotamia, they never went back home again; but they were always worried that the people they encountered in Canaan or Egypt for that matter would treat them badly.[54] This is a feeling and concern found among many African immigrants discussed in this chapter. However, Baden, commenting on Genesis 12:10–20, says that although Abraham and his family, who were strangers in strange lands, were at the mercy of foreign kings, they were treated with respect. Genesis 20:15 states: "And Abimelech said, 'Here, my land is before you; settle wherever you please.'" Then in Genesis 26:11 Abimelech is reported as charging all the people, saying, "Anyone who molests this man [Abraham] or his wife shall be put to death." Clearly, Abraham and his people were not only respected; they were also protected. This is an experience many African immigrants wish they had.

Peter C. Phan contends that Abraham, because of his wealth and power, could have easily settled down in any city or in one of the many little kingdoms of his choice and become a permanent and "preeminent citizen." However, argues Phan, "Abraham intentionally chose a migratory way of life for himself and his family, erecting tents as temporary dwellings, rather than being incorporated into the local communities."[55] There is a significant difference here with African immigrants in that Abraham chose to remain a migrant and live a migratory life. African immigrants who come to the United States chose to settle here and seek to become permanent residents and citizens. Unlike the African immigrants, however, Abraham is like the Euro-American multinational corporation executives who have apartments all over the world and can live in New York, London, Paris, Johannesburg, Rio de Janeiro, Seoul, Tokyo, Nairobi, Addis Ababa, Beijing, Accra, or Lagos, etc., without needing to become citizens of these countries.

However, despite these differences, there are more parallels between Abraham's experience and African immigrants' realities. Prior to the subsequent accumulation of wealth and eventual prosperity, Abraham and Sarah's story, like the stories of most African immigrants, is a story of struggle, survival, and endurance in the quest for comfort and stability. Kathleen M. O'Connor suggests that most stories in the book of Genesis are accounts of survival struggles of people. She goes on to argue that we view the book of Genesis itself as "survival literature."[56] In Genesis the ancestors are strangers and migrants from beginning to end, who are grappling with disasters and profound worries about their survival in the face of existential challenges. She writes: "Genesis contains stories of catastrophe after catastrophe and . . . the promises which structure the ancestral chapters (12–50) respond to deep anxieties about the [people's existential realities]." She adds that "God's promises to Abraham and his family relate not only to drama in the lives of the ancestors, but also, and perhaps primarily, to the reading audience that still lives in great trepidation about its future."[57] Concerns for their future are clearly reasons that motivate many African immigrants to come to the United States in search of better educational prospects and job opportunities.

Analyzing Abraham's migration through the perspective of work, the Theology of Work Project (POW) Bible Commentary on Genesis suggests that the story of Abraham and Sarah is perfused with work.[58] At every point, Abraham and Sarah and their people "struggle to make a living, endure social upheaval, raise children in safety, and remain faithful to God in the midst of a broken world, much as we do today." This commentary describes Abraham as a vulnerable economic migrant who was fleeing starvation and had to lie several times in order to survive.[59]

One of the insights we can gain from the migratory life of Abraham and his people is that migration is as old as the human family itself. People have always been on the move, and for various reasons. We humans are a migratory species. But migration or immigration is a major life change which can be very stressful. Regardless of the reasons why people migrate or relocate to another country, everyone experiences loss and grief as part of the migratory process. Understanding these dynamics of loss and grief related to immigration can help us appreciate the difficulties and struggles inherent in immigration and the challenges involved in the process of adaptation to the new situation, while developing awareness that, in most cases, the process of adaptation can be hard and may take a lot of time and effort.

Even though we find some parallels between Abraham's story and the stories of African immigrants, it might be helpful to note with Dube that "the Abraham story may conceal a number of social issues, for instance, how many years did Abraham take to settle in the land, what social and identity conflict did Abraham face from the locals?" Dube suggests that a glimpse on these questions is given in Genesis 13, when Abraham's shepherds quarreled with Lot's shepherds. Although these fights may be viewed as signs of internal conflicts within the household or larger extended family, Dube's point is really helpful here as he notes that if such domestic disputes erupted among Abraham's people, "it is possible that similar quarrels over grazing the land could have arisen with other herdsmen in the region."[60]

Framing Migratory Grief and Cultural Melancholia

Although many of the issues and challenges experienced by African immigrants and Abraham and Sarah have not been framed in terms of grief and loss, the immigration/migration processes they went through clearly reflect significant grief and losses, and as such point to the need to look at migration or immigration as an experience of loss and grief. In some immigration cases, the disruption is so strong and violent that the experience of adaptation and adjustment becomes in and of itself an experience of trauma.[61] For the purposes of this chapter, we will focus on framing the immigration experience as an experience of loss and grief—that is, the immigration experience as an experience of migratory grief and cultural bereavement.

So, what is migratory grief? Before discussing what migratory grief is, let me first describe what grief is, broadly speaking. Grief is a painful, complex, and universal experience occasioned by loss, death, and/or separation from a loved person, object, or the environment. Mitchell and Anderson suggest that "grief is the normal but bewildering cluster of ordinary human emotions arising in response to a significant loss, intensified and complicated by the relationship to the person or the lost object."[62] There are multiple expressions and dimensions of grief including the emotional, cognitive, and behavioral dynamics and processes of loss and grief, bereavement, mourning, normal and atypical grief; and there are cultural and ethnic variations in grieving. It is important to note here that grief and loss not related to death could be just as devastating to a person or community as the grief related to the death of a loved one. The immigration process can be an experience of loss and grief as it might involve not only losing connections to the country of origin and the communities and people that have shaped and sustained the immigrant, but also a disruption of a person's core narrative about themselves and their life. Immigration can also involve the loss of the very thing one is immigrating for—that is, the dream and vision for the future, and the coherent narrative that can sustain and guide our goals and educational and professional pursuits.[63] Thus, a broader view of grief can help us understand ways in which the immigration experience is replete with losses and grief.

So grief is a response to losses that are both related to death and not related to death, both tangible and intangible in their description. An individual does not have to lose a loved one to death in order to grieve; grief can occur after a loved one with advanced dementia is placed in a long-term care facility, with the ending of an intimate relationship, with the loss of hopes and dreams, and with the loss of self that may accompany life-altering events. Grief is viewed as an adaptive response to experiences that challenge our assumptions about how the world should work, and how we view ourselves and others within that world.[64]

This broader view of grief is helpful as we examine the various expressions of loss and grief as reflected in the immigration process of African immigrants, as well as the migration experience of Abraham and Sarah as discussed in this chapter. Understanding grief is helpful in gaining insights not only into the pain and suffering caused by the various changes that accompany the immigration experience, but also insights into human beings' ability to connect with their inner resources and resources within their environment that help them appreciate their strength, innate resilience, and capacity to heal in relationship with others, in community.

The above discussion helps us to see that there are different kinds of losses. These have been helpfully classified into six types of loss by Mitchell and Anderson: 1) material loss is the loss of a physical object or of familiar surroundings to which one has a significant attachment; 2) relationship loss is the ending of opportunities to relate to someone and no longer being able to be emotionally or physically present with them; 3) intrapsychic loss is loss of an image or internal representation of a dream, an idea, or a vision; 4) functional loss has to do with muscular or neurological functions of the body such as losing eye sight, hearing, amputation of a limb, or loss of mental awareness; 5) role loss is a loss of a specific social role like in retirement, divorce, promotion, or moving; 6) systemic loss involves collective loss of someone or something important to the system, group, or community.[65] Many of these losses happen in the process of leaving one's country of origin and moving to the receiving country. The various forms of loss come to encompass material loss of familiar surroundings and the environment; loss of the multiple relationships that have nurtured and sustained the immigrant; loss of the image of oneself in relationship to the people and the country of origin; loss of the earlier dreams of seeing oneself living in a particular place, building a home, or envisioning oneself living in a home in which one grew up; loss of one's role in relation to the community, and perhaps to the family concerning the day to day functioning; and systemic loss with regard to lack of participation in the life of the group, community, or family due to physical absence.

The stories of Lombe Mwembo, Omiunota Ukpokodu, Nonye Obiora, Francis Musoni, other (African) immigrants, as well as Abraham and Sarah embody all these various types of losses. Mwembo, for example, grieved the loss of his professional self by accepting the security guard position. He also grieved the self he was in the Congo and his self-identity as a teacher, former school principal, and former manager of a nonprofit. Related to this role was the systemic loss of a supportive, respectful, and loving community. His process of adapting and adjusting to the United States also caused him to grieve deeply the loss of the image he had of this country as a place of justice, diversity, and equity. He saw these values as being out of reach in his quest for a professional job. Mwembo and his colleagues did not anticipate running into situations where their skin color and place of origin and accent would become obstacles to professional development and access to a stable and good paying job.

As noted above, loss is unavoidable in human life, let alone in the immigration process. As such grief as a natural response to the universality of loss challenges us to acknowledge the painful experiences we go through in life. Not only does this reality challenge us to recognize the pain and suffering we go through, but it also invites us to grieve. And grieving allows us to process the emotions and thoughts related to the loss, accept the change, and be ready to move to a new phase of life as we integrate the losses and grow in our ability to live with the struggles and complexities of life. Immigration is a stressful life event that brings massive changes in the immigrant's life. The process of adaptation and adjustment to these changes is where the meaning-making and work of pastoral care need to take place in helping people to adapt and adjust to their new reality.

Even though Abraham and Sarah's story does not specifically identify their grief experiences, we can attempt to identify some of the grief and loss they went through during their journey from Ur of the Chaldeans to the land of Canaan based on the typology of loss discussed above. The biblical text specifically identifies several deaths in Abraham's family. These include the death of Haran, Abraham's brother and father of Lot; the death of Terah, Abraham's father (and yes Sarah's father as well!); and the death of Sarah and Abraham themselves, among others. Although some of these deaths are not necessarily or directly related to the migration process per se, they are nevertheless important losses that may have even propelled the family to leave Ur of the Chaldeans (in the case of the death of Haran), leave Haran (in the case of Terah's death). In the case of Sarah's death, we are told that Abraham "went in to mourn for Sarah and to weep for her" (Genesis 23:2). Here Abraham experienced relational loss and role loss as a husband. This might give us some hints about grief and loss in Sarah when they went to Egypt and she was "coached" to say she was Abraham's sister. Even though the text is silent on her feelings, we can infer some deep sense of not only relationship loss in relation to Abraham, but also role loss as his wife (although this was regained after Sarah was rescued by God); there is also intrapsychic loss here in terms of Sarah's self-perception and self-identity. This loss is directly related to the migratory process as Abraham and Sarah are trying to ensure their survival in the face of stressful changes. Certainly, there is also loss of homeland (material loss), social status, and the struggle to keep alive the dream and hopes related to the promises and blessings of God during their several moves from Ur of the Chaldeans to Haran, to Shechem, from there to Bethel, Egypt, to Hebron, to Gerar, and moving back and forth between these and other locations. In the process they lose connections with communities, relatives, and places. The migratory life of Abraham and Sarah feels really dizzy!

Having said all this, we can thus define migratory grief as a "phenomenon that occurs as a result of migration/immigration, is accompanied by stressors related to the loss of the home country and adjustment to the new country, both of which entail the change of self-identity and growth."[66] This definition provides a good foundation for thinking about the insights we need to harness to think about pastoral care and the support for those dealing with migratory grief. Before we move to the next section, let me say a word on cultural melancholia or cultural bereavement, two terms that I am using interchangeably in this chapter.

Merriam-Webster defines melancholia as severe depression characterized especially by profound sadness, or a sad quality or mood. Sigmund Freud described melancholia as mournful and depressive feelings and thoughts.[67] The DSM-V-TR terminology and criteria for this condition would describe this as a major depressive episode.[68] But this is not what I want to convey by the term cultural melancholia. What I want to communicate by this term is the distress and saddening recollection of practices, values, and worldview that used to provide a sense of grounding, guidance, and practical wisdom about life, relationships, and meaning, but that is no longer available in the new environment. For example, some of the African immigrants discussed in this paper recall how they used to be treated with respect as elders in their own communities in their country of origin. Young people in their country of origin showed deference toward them, would not say mean or disrespectful words to them, or ridicule them. But their accounts about their experience in the American school systems are the opposite of what they knew and how they were treated in their country of origin.

Indeed, cultural melancholia then seeks to recognize the loss of one's culture of origin and express a deep yearning for it. It recognizes that the loss of one's culture and social structure can cause a normal grief reaction, without pathologizing the grief being expressed over that loss. As Dinesh Bhugra and Matthew A. Becker suggest, "migration involves the loss of the familiar, including language (especially colloquial and dialect), attitudes, values, social structures and support networks." Grieving for this loss needs to be viewed as a healthy reaction and a natural consequence of migration.[69] In this sense, cultural melancholia is not a dysfunction of an individual but a persistent and enduring yearning for the cultural heritage that has been lost or is in the process of being lost. As such, the sorrow and long-lasting yearning for their culture of origin as expressed in the accounts of African immigrants and in the story of Abraham and Sarah is a normal phenomenon and response to migratory losses.[70]

However, there is an aspect of social melancholia we need to deal with, especially because of its relationship to race. Most immigrants of color in the United States are always confronted with a critical question and decision to make, namely the question about whether they would be willing to give up their cultural and ethnic heritage to identify with and assimilate into the dominant American culture or resist assimilation and risk further marginalization and racism.[71] Korean American practical theologian Choi Hee An has written about the struggles non-white immigrants go through as they seek to fully become part of the American society. She points out how the dominant white culture evokes in non-white immigrants an urgent need and desire to adopt American white culture without analyzing the toxic and racist manipulation involved in the process of assimilation where they not only experience discrimination but also simultaneously feel accepted, rejected, adopted, resisted, and influenced by the dominant American white culture.[72] Research with Asian Americans and Asian immigrants suggests that immigration, assimilation, and racialization are all significant losses that should be mourned but too often are repressed instead.[73] The internalization of these repressed feelings and thoughts negatively manifests as racial melancholia, an internalized conflict of identity propelled by a search for acceptance into the dominant culture. By seeking to be accepted into the dominant white culture, people must disassociate themselves consciously or unconsciously from their cultural heritage and history. The resulting racial dissociation is used "to negotiate losses associated with the politics of immigration, assimilation, and racialization and, in particular, to navigate opposing realities of colorblindness."[74] The result is an ongoing struggle with one's identity and nonresolution of the losses and grief involved in this process. Needless to say, racial melancholia does not facilitate adaptive assimilation that is respectful of one's cultural identity, heritage, and history.

Insights for Pastoral Care: The Tasks of Mourning and the Role of the Church

How can pastors and churches help (African) immigrants find meaningful connections and supportive community, and be able to move forward with resilience and strength? We need to pay attention to the acculturation, adaptation, and adjustment processes—and to insights from the determination, resilience, and hope of Abraham and Sarah. Worden's work can be very helpful here.

Worden's task-based model of grief and mourning provides a helpful template for understanding the experience of grief and, although he focuses on the grief related to death, his tasks of mourning can be applied to the losses experienced in the immigration process. The model also does not pathologize grief but sees it as a normal response or reaction to significant loss. What is particularly helpful about using this model with immigrants is that his tasks of mourning describe the mourning process as an active and intentional effort to take action and do something about the pain and suffering caused by loss. In that sense, this is an empowering approach for immigrants because it gives the mourner some sense of leverage and hope that there is something he or she can actively do to adapt to the loss.[75] His definition of mourning as the adaptation to loss leads him to outline four basic tasks of mourning.[76]

To accept the reality of loss, which involves recognizing that the loss has happened and that it's real. The situation has changed.

To process the pain of grief. This involves acknowledging and working through the pain associated with the loss.

To adjust to a world without what has been lost. Here Worden describes three areas of adjustment that need to be addressed: external adjustments, or how the loss affects one's everyday functioning in the world; internal adjustments, which have to do with how the loss affects one's sense of self, or identity; and spiritual adjustments, which examine how the loss affects one's beliefs, values, and assumptions about the world. Basically, adjustment emphasizes the need to relearn the world after the loss and develop new ways of dealing with the world.

To find a way to remember what has been lost while embarking on the rest of one's journey through life. It is important to note here that the bond with the lost object changes but continues and, like the bond, the process of grief does not end but instead changes over time. This is an important insight which requires a lot of patience and grace to be able to navigate these changes and be able to regain perspective and find a meaningful and life-giving re-orientation to life.

Understanding and honoring this process of grieving is really critical for pastors, other pastoral caregivers, and their congregations, as they journey with people who are grappling with migratory grief and loss. An important reminder about this model is that it is broad and non-liner, and is thus better able to accommodate the uniqueness of individuals' experiences and approaches to grief.

The role of the church is important here. Pastoral leaders who have this understanding of grief can be very helpful to those who struggle with migratory grief and loss. Indeed, when immigrants are going through all these experiences of loss, belonging to a loving church community that recognizes their struggles and stands with them to provide a holding place and caring space can make a big difference. Reading Abraham's story side by side with the immigration experience of Africans suggests the need for informed conversation within the churches regarding the challenges and suffering experienced by African immigrants in the United States in the forms of migratory grief and cultural melancholia. The implications for pastoral care suggest the need to acknowledge the losses, name the pain related to these losses, mourn the losses, and create communities of mourning that are empathic and supportive.

Indeed, the congregation that is attuned to the mourning of its immigrant members can be a welcoming, caring, and sustaining place where immigrants who feel isolated and alone can receive a special social and relational grace that renews their basic trust and revives their faith in the God of life, who calls them to the fullness of life even in the midst of challenging circumstances that seem to be devoid of grace. The congregation can be a place of hope where people who are agonizing under the weight of migratory grief can realize that they are not alone. But this requires pastors and congregations to develop the ability to empathize, to show love and care—not in a condescending or intrusive way, but with pastoral sensibilities that are nurturing and affirming of the dignity of those who are the recipients of pastoral support. Being aware of the challenges and struggles immigrants encounter in this country can make a big difference in this direction. Perhaps many African immigrants prefer to attend and participate in immigrant led churches because of the desire to be treated with respect and dignity even in moments of significant vulnerability related to their immigration experience.[77]

Beyond the pastoral and community conversations where pastors and their people offer support as they learn about the challenges immigrants face socially and professionally, it would be helpful to be intentional about including in our liturgies and acts of worship readings, prayers, sermons and bible studies that show awareness about the immigrant experience, particularly as it relates to matters of race and ethnicity, and to be clear about our commitments for justice as we seek to listen, learn, and grow together as people of faith. Congregations should act as a pilgrim people who are journeying together in search of "the city that is [yet] to come" (Hebrews 13:14), and in the company of the pilgrim God who is journeying with us.

Dealing with migratory grief and cultural bereavement alone can cause significant emotional exhaustion. This is why the church, even as a community of strangers, can be a holding place and a sustaining presence for those who are agonizing under the weight of isolating grief and loss

Conclusion

I have attempted in this chapter to uncover the migratory grief and cultural melancholia African immigrants experience in the United States and to relate that experience to the grief and loss in the migratory experience of Abraham and Sarah. In doing so, I have tried to achieve three things. First, I have tried to describe and explain the struggles and challenges African immigrants encounter in their new home in the form of migratory grief and loss. Second, I have attempted to relate these experiences to the migratory experiences of Abraham and Sarah, to show that migration and the quest for home is as old as the human experience itself. Third, I have tried to identify the nature of the grief and loss African immigrants experience, and the existential threat these experiences represent. I have argued that for pastors and churches to be able to help African immigrants find meaningful connections and supportive communities, they need to understand the acculturation, adaptation, and adjustment processes of African immigrants. Doing so would empower pastors and churches to build empathic communities that attend to the powerful and isolating pain of loss involved in the immigration experience and, in the process, the church will become truly a holding place and sustaining presence for those who are agonizing under the weight of isolating grief and loss.

Discussion Questions

- In what ways is the immigration experience of African immigrants a pastoral care issue? Why should congregations in general, and Black churches in particular, attend to this issue?
- How does your local church community think, feel, and act toward African immigrants?
- What specific actions might you take to listen to, learn from, and be in solidarity with immigrants of African descent in general, and African immigrants in particular?
- As a Black Christian, what difference does it make to read Abraham's story as a story of a vulnerable economic migrant who moved several times from one place to another because of existential threats and environmental reasons? How does this understanding inform your practices of care?

Resources for Further Reading

Denise Dombkowski Hopkins, and Michael S. Koppel, *Grounded in the Living Word: The Old Testament and Pastoral Care Practices* (Eerdmans Publishing, 2010). Especially Chapter 5: "Pain, Grief, and Lament," and Chapter 7: "Covenant Care Community."

Tapiwa N. Mucherera, *Counseling and Pastoral Care in African and Other Cross-Cultural Contexts* (Wipf & Stock Publishers, 2017).

Tapiwa N. Mucherera et al., eds., *Tri-level Identity Crisis: Children of First-Generation Immigrants* (Pickwick Publications, 2020).

Hugh R. Page Jr., ed., *The Africana Bible: Reading Israel's Scriptures from Africa and the African Diaspora*. 2nd ed. Fortress Press, 2024.

Endnotes

1 Salem Solomon, "African Immigrant Population on Rise in US," *Voice of America*, February 17, 2017, https://www.voanews.com/a/african-immigrant-population-on-the-rise-in-us/3728715.html/.

2 Lombe L. Mwembo, "My African Skin Color Weighs More Than My U.S. Degrees: In the Eyes of U.S. Children and School Leaders," in *Reprocessing Race, Language and Ability: African-Born Educators and Students in Transnational America*, ed. Immaculée Harushimana et al. (Peter Lang, 2013), 186.

3 For details on factors that have contributed to the social, economic, and political instability in DR Congo, see, for example, M. Fulgence Nyengele, "Healing Postcolonial Trauma in the African Experience: The Case of DR Congo," in *Pastoral Care, Health, Healing, and Wholeness in African Contexts: Methodology, Context, and Issues*, ed. Tapiwa N. Mucherera and Emmanuel Y. Lartey (Wipf & Stock Publishers, 2017).

4 Mwembo, "My African Skin Color Weighs More Than My U.S. Degrees," 186.

5 Mwembo, "My African Skin Color Weighs More Than My U.S. Degrees," 186–87.

6 There are many underemployed immigrants with college degrees in the United States. The concept often referred to as "brain waste" addresses this pervasive reality of underemployment among immigrants in general, and African and other ethnic immigrants in particular. Batalova and Fix of the Migration Policy Institute write that 21 percent of college-educated immigrants are either unemployed or working in jobs that require no more than a high school diploma. They write that "while most states have seen their college-educated immigrant populations grow since 2010, there have been few strategic efforts to improve the integration prospects of the new immigrants . . . The states and the nation are failing to fully leverage the skills that millions of college-educated immigrants have to offer." Batalova and Fix go on to observe that there are stark patterns of racial and ethnic disadvantages that emerge in the underemployment of both highly skilled immigrants and US born. See Batalova and Fix, *Leaving Money on the Table: The Persistence of Brain Waste Among College-Educated Immigrants* (Migration Policy Institute, June 2021), 1, https://www.migrationpolicy.org/research/

brain-waste-college-educated-immigrants. On the plight of Black and Latino immigrants and US born, see also an article by the Migration Policy Institute, "Black and Latino Graduates, Immigrant and U.S. Born Alike, Face Greater Risk of Skill Underutilization than White Counterparts, MPI Analysis Finds," June 9, 2021, https://www.migrationpolicy.org/news/immigrant-skill-underutilization-race-ethnicity-state-analysis .

7 See Fraternel D. Amuri Misako, *The Brain Waste of Foreign-Educated Professionals in the United States: Employment Profiles and Policy Issues Versus Community Capitals* (Éditions Universitaires Européennes, 2018).

8 Mwembo, "My African Skin Color Weighs More Than My U.S. Degrees," 189.

9 Mwembo, "My African Skin Color Weighs More Than My U.S. Degrees," 190.

10 Lombe L. Mwembo, "Congolese Immigrants' Perception About Their Children's Education in Philadelphia" (Unpublished PhD diss., Temple University, 2009), iv.

11 Mwembo, "Congolese Immigrants' Perception," iv.

12 Immaculée Harushimana et al., eds., *Reprocessing Race, Language and Ability: African-Born Educators and Students in Transnational America* (Peter Lang, 2013).

13 It is important to note, however, that some studies have found that there are significant differences among African immigrants, depending on factors related to pre-immigration characteristics and class and their impact on their integration into the US society. These differences were specifically observed among Nigerian-born and Somali-born immigrants in the way that they integrate into the US society. For example, Abel Chikanda and Julie Susanne Morris suggest that we reconsider the treatment of African immigrants as a collective group as this obscures differences between immigrants from different African countries and the way they adjust to life in the United States. See Chikanda and Morris, "Assessing the Integration Outcomes of African Immigrants in the United States," *African Geographical Review* 40, no. 1 (2021): https://doi.org/10.1080/19376812.2020.1744455.

14 Omiunota N. Ukpokodu, "Foreword," in *Reprocessing Race, Language and Ability: African-Born Educators and Students in Transnational America*, ed. Immaculée Harushimana et al. (Peter Lang, 2013), xvi.

15 Ibid., xviii.

16 Ibid., xix.

17 Ibid., xx.

18 There are twenty-eight nations represented by African immigrants in this book: Algeria, Botswana, Burundi, Cameroon, Cote d'Ivoire/Ivory Coast, DR Congo, Egypt, Ethiopia, The Gambia, Ghana, Guinea, Kenya, Liberia, Libya, Malawi, Namibia, Nigeria, Republic of Congo, Rwanda, Senegal, Sierra Leone, Somalia, South Africa, South Sudan, Tanzania, Uganda, Zambia, and Zimbabwe. See Francis Musoni et al., *Voices of African Immigrants in Kentucky: Migration, Identity, and Transnationality* (University Press of Kentucky, 2019), vii.

19 Musoni et al., *Voices of African Immigrants in Kentucky*, 2019.

20 Immaculée Harushimana, "A New Perspective on the Assimilation and Adaptation of African-Born Immigrants," in Harushimana, *Reprocessing Race*, 236.

21 The APA Presidential Task Force on Immigration "Crossroads: The Psychology of Immigration in the New Century," *Journal of Latina/o Psychology* 1, no. 3 (2012), 3, https://doi.org/10.1037/lat0000001.

22 Nonye C. Obiora, "Foreign or Funny; Not Inferior: An African Educator Navigates Invisible Barriers in Teaching," in Harushimana *Reprocessing Race*, 214.

23 Ibid.

24 Ibid., 215.

25 The APA Presidential Task Force on Immigration, "Crossroads," 1–2.

26 Teresa Wiltz, "For Some Black Immigrants, Life in Limbo," *Stateline*, September 27, 2017, https://www.pewtrusts.org/en/research-and-analysis/blogs/stateline/2017/09/27/for-some-black-immigrants-life-in-limbo.

27 Wiltz, "Some Black Immigrants," 2.

28 Danae King, "Ohio's African Immigrant Community Growing in Size, Diversity, and Impact," *The Columbus Dispatch*, February 12, 2019.

29 King, "Ohio's African Immigrant Community," 2.

30 Njeri M. Clement, "Home Away from Home: Experiences of African Women Immigrants Living in Minnesota" (master's thesis, St. Cloud State University, December 2017), 8–9, St. Cloud State Repository.

31 For a thorough discussion of sexism in African cultures and efforts for reform and transformation, see M. Fulgence Nyengele, *African Women's Theology, Gender Relations, and Family Systems Theory: Pastoral Theological Considerations, and Guidelines for Care and Counseling* (Peter Lang, 2004); see also Mercy Amba Oduyoye, *Introducing African Women's Theology* (Pilgrim Press, 2001).

32 For a very helpful discussion of research findings on the blindness to gender-based violence toward women in migration studies in the fields of psychology, economics, sociology, and anthropology, see Pamela Cooper-White, "Women Migrants, Gender-Based Trauma and Spiritual Care," in *Pastoral and Spiritual Care Across Religions and Cultures II: Spiritual Care and Migration*, ed. Isabelle Noth and Claudia Kohli Reichenbach (Vandenhoeck & Ruprecht, 2019); the Report of the APA Presidential Task Force on Immigration also decries the fact that the unique challenges women and girls face in the migratory process and their particular needs and experiences are overlooked and unrecognized in both the research scholarship and treatment interventions. See "Crossroads," 32–33.

33 Cooper-White, "Women Migrants, Gender-Based Trauma and Spiritual Care," 17–18.

34 Clement, "Home Away from Home," 9.

35 Clement, "Home Away from Home," 9–10.

36 Clement, "Home Away from Home," 18–21.

37 Mary Johnson Osirim, "African Women in the New Diaspora: Transnationalism and the (Re) Creation of Home," *African and Asian Studies* 7, 2008: 367–97.

38 Unless indicated otherwise, all Bible quotations are from the New Revised Standard Version (NRSV) of the Bible.

39 See, for example, Romans 4:3–12; James 2:21–24; Hebrews 11:17–19.

40 Zorodzai Dube, "Abraham and Jesus as Ancient Migrants: An African Migration Perspective," Perichoresis 14, no. 1 (2016): 63–75, https://doi.org/10.1515/perc-2016-0004.

41 Dube, "Abraham and Jesus as Ancient Migrants," 5.

42 Dube, "Abraham and Jesus as Ancient Migrants," 5.

43 Keith N. Grüneberg, *Abraham, Blessing and the Nations* (Walter de Gruyter, 2003), 161.

44 Jonathan Grossman, *Abram to Abraham: A Literary Analysis of the Abraham Narrative* (Peter Lang, 2016), 79.
45 Grüneberg, *Abraham, Blessing and the Nations*, 159.
46 Grossman, *Abram to Abraham*, 86.
47 Grüneberg, *Abraham, Blessing and the Nations*, 154.
48 Grossman, *Abram to Abraham*, 97.
49 Ibid., 146.
50 Ibid., 92–93.
51 Megan Warner, *Re-Imagining Abraham: A Re-Assessment of the Influence of Deuteronomism in Genesis* (Brill, 2018), 83.
52 Karen Quan et al., "Acculturative Stress: How to Help Immigrant Students," *Psychiatric Times* 39, no. 9 (2022): 15–17.
53 David Carr, *Holy Resilience: The Bible's Traumatic Origins* (Yale University Press, 2014), 100.
54 Joel Baden, "The Bible and Immigration," virtual lecture, posted January 31, 2017, by Yale Divinity School, YouTube, 44:45, https://youtu.be/vTsWnvnn8zQ.
55 Peter C. Phan, "God, the Beginning and the End of Migration: A Theology of God from the Experience and Perspective of Migrants," in *Christian Theology in the Age of Migration: Implications for World Christianity*, ed. Peter C. Phan (Lexington Books, 2020), 106.
56 Kathleen M. O'Connor, "Stammering Toward the Unsayable: Old Testament Theology, Trauma, and Genesis," *Interpretation: A Journal of Bible and Theology* 70, no. 3 (2016): 305; for more details on this, see Kathleen M. O'Connor, Genesis (Smyth & Helwys Publishing, 2018).
57 O'Connor, "Stammering Toward the Unsayable," 306.
58 "Bible Commentary: Genesis 12–50 and Work," Theology of Work Project, accessed August 26, 2021, https://www.theologyofwork.org/old-testament/genesis-12-50-and-work.
59 Ibid.
60 Dube, "Abraham and Jesus as Ancient Migrants," 68.
61 RoseMarie Perez Foster, "When Immigration Is Trauma: Guidelines for the Individual and Family Clinician," *American Journal of Orthopsychiatry* 71, no. 2 (2001).
62 Kenneth R. Mitchell and Herbert Anderson, *All Our Losses, All Our Griefs: Resources for Pastoral Care* (Westminster John Knox, 1983), 54.

63 For a discussion about how our past and present narratives can open up or limit positive possibilities for the future, see Andrew Lester, *Hope in Pastoral Care and Counseling* (Westminster John Knox Press, 1995), 45.

64 Howard R. Winokuer and Darcy L. Harris, *Principles and Practices of Grief Counseling* (Springer Publishing Company, 2012), x.

65 Mitchell and Anderson, *All Our Losses, All Our Griefs*, 36–46.

66 Adapted from Emilia Grycuk, "The Impact of the Difference in Individualism, Acculturation, and Gender on Migratory Grief and Psychological Well-Being: A Cultural Comparison" (master's thesis, Universiteit Utrecht, 2020).

67 Tormod Knutsen, "The Dynamics of Grief and Melancholia," *Tidsskr Nor Legeforen* 140, no. 5 (2020), https://doi.org/10.4045/tidsskr.19.0504.

68 *Diagnostic and Statistical Manual of Mental Disorders: DSM-5* (American Psychiatric Publishing, 2013).

69 Dinesh Bhugra and Matthew A. Becker, "Migration, Cultural Bereavement and Cultural Identity," *World Psychiatry: Official Journal of the World Psychiatric Association* 4, no. 1 (2005): 18–24.

70 In the case of Abraham and Sarah the flawed assumptions Abraham had about other cultures with regard to his own safety might be construed as unconscious expressions of his yearning for his familiar cultural assumptions and practices; he also yearns for his original culture when, before dying, he commissioned one of his most trusted servants to go back to his (Abraham's) people to find a wife for his son Isaac.

71 Ester R. Shapiro, "Grief in Family and Cultural Context: Learning from Latino Families," *Cultural Diversity and Mental Health* 1, no. 2 (1995): 162.

72 Choi Hee An, *A Postcolonial Self: Korean Immigrant Theology and Church* (SUNY Press, 2015), 3–4; see also M. Fulgence Nyengele, "Review of *A Postcolonial Self: Korean Immigrant Theology and Church*, by Choi Hee An," *Journal of Pastoral Theology* 26, no, 1, (2016): 72–74.

73 David L. Eng and Shinhee Han, *Racial Melancholia, Racial Dissociation: On the Social and Psychic Lives of Asian Americans* (Duke University Press, 2019), 3.

74 Eng and Han, *Racial Melancholia, Racial Dissociation*, 105.

75 I have adapted the language in these tasks to make them relevant for migratory loss and grief that is not related to the loss associated with death.

76 See J. William Worden, *Grief Counseling and Grief Therapy: A Handbook for the Mental Health Practitioner* (Springer Publishing Company, 2018), 41–53.

77 Adebayo Oyebade, "African Immigrants and their Churches," in *The New African Diaspora in the United States*, ed. Adebayo Oyebade and Toyin Falola (Routledge, 2017); see also Frieder Ludwig and J. Kwabena Asamoah-Gyadu eds., *The African Christian Presence in the West: New Immigrant Congregations and Transnational Networks in North America and Europe* (Africa World Press, 2011).

3

All God's Children: Grief as a Reconciliatory Agent in 2 Samuel 21:1-14

Terry Ann Smith
and Micah McCreary

On a hot summer night in August of 1955, fourteen-year-old African American, Emmett Till, was removed from his relatives' home in Mississippi by two white men. He was taken to a barn, stripped naked, pistol-whipped, and then shot in the head. The perpetrators tied a seventy-five–pound cotton gin fan around his neck with barbwire and dumped his lifeless body in the Tallahatchie River. His crime, according to his killers, was that he whistled at a white woman. Emmett Till's body was returned to his mother in Chicago and upon witnessing the extent of the brutality enacted on the bloated unrecognizable corpse of her son, Mamie Till-Mobley refused attempts to bury him quietly. Insisting on an open casket ceremony, she said, "Let the people see what they did to my boy."[1] With the recent popularity of television in the 1950s, she would guarantee that what was done in the rural South would be viewed in living rooms across America, influencing public opinion. Mamie Till-Mobley was persistent as she submerged her own grief while contemplating a decision to boldly stand against the systemic injustices that had brought her (and her son) to that point. Putting the disfigured body of Emmett Till on display to the entire world would shame a nation and usher in the Civil Rights Movement. The persons who killed her son were acquitted, and while they later admitted to the crime, they managed to elude justice not once, but twice. Mamie Till-Mobley died in 2003, never fully reconciled to the events surrounding her son's death or those who were responsible for it. In 2 Samuel 21:1–14, we find a story that prefigures the tragedy of Emmett Till. It is the story of another grieving mother, Rizpah. This mother, like Mamie Till-Mobley, does for her sons in death what she cannot do for them in life; that is, protect them from predators.

Rationalizing the Irrational

> Now there was a famine in the days of David for three years, year after year; and David inquired of the LORD. The LORD said, 'There is bloodguilt on Saul and on his house because he put the Gibeonites to death.' So the king called the Gibeonites and spoke to them. (Now the Gibeonites were not of the people of Israel, but of the remnant of the Amorites; although the people of Israel had sworn to spare them, Saul had tried to wipe them out in his zeal for the people of Israel and Judah). David said to the Gibeonites, 'What shall I do for you? How shall I make expiation, that you may bless the heritage of the LORD?' The Gibeonites said to him, 'It is not a matter of silver or gold between us and Saul or his house; neither is it for us to put anyone to death in Israel.' He said, 'What do you say that I should do for you?' They said to the

> king, 'The man who consumed us and planned to destroy us, so that we should have no place in all the territory of Israel— let seven of his sons be handed over to us, and we will impale them before the Lord at Gibeon on the mountain of the Lord.' The king said, 'I will hand them over.' (2 Samuel 21:1–6)

2 Samuel 21 begins with a food shortage brought about by a famine, which plagued the land for three years. The scarcity, national in scope, caused King David to "inquire of the LORD" of its origins. The problem, according to the LORD, was the bloodguilt of King Saul (now deceased) and his house who "put the Gibeonites to death" (2 Samuel 21:1). This rationale, under the guise of reconciliation, leads King David to approach the Gibeonites and inquire what he can do for them to "bless the heritage of the LORD," meaning David, the land, and the people of Judah (21:3). Notably, the king never mentions Saul by name, or the offense proffered in 21:1. The Gibeonites (who are not Israelites according to 21:2) respond in 21:5 using the Levitical law of *lex talionis*, also known as the law of retaliation justice (Leviticus 24:17–22) against Saul, and since Saul is no longer living, against his descendants. Most commentators point to Joshua 9 as the backdrop for this accusation which recounts a negotiated truce between the Gibeonites and the Israelites. Yet, there is no textual evidence outside of 2 Samuel 21 that supports the claim in 21:1 or 21:5 that Saul violates this agreement or attempts to eradicate this group.[2]

Framed as an act of restitution, David honors the Gibeonites' request to impale seven of Saul's male descendants and hands over two of Saul's sons and five of his grandsons (2 Samuel 21:6, 8). Only, the son of Jonathan, Mephibosheth, is spared (21:7). All seven of them are ritually slaughtered and their corpses left exposed on a hill (21:9, 10). Cheryl Exum asserts, "whereas ritual execution like that described here constituted punishment for treaty violation in the ancient near east, the disrespect of the elemental right of the dead to burial poses a serious problem. Can the natural order, the end of the famine and the renewal of nature, be reestablished by an act against the dead that violates the natural order."[3] The event is bloody and shameful without regard for the mothers who must look upon the mutilated bodies of their children. The violent nature of the event and the public display of mutilated corpses would serve as a warning that others would suffer a similar fate should they choose to defy the king or his allies. The execution takes place "before the Lord," bringing into sharp focus the use of religion to authorize what could be characterized as a government-sanctioned execution. South African anti-apartheid activist Allan Boesak submits, "this is what happens when you rise up against the king, or when you displease the palace, when you question the powerful, or when you bring the security of the state in danger. Looking at those bodies on the trees, this is what the people see: a ritual killing, done 'before the Lord,' required by the Lord. They also see a political killing, a public execution with a lesson for all."[4] Walter Brueggemann characterizes David as a "ruthless opportunist who found a way to eliminate the Saulide threat, and to do so in the guise of religious legitimacy and political necessity."[5]

Here, one questions whether national or personal interests are served by David's actions. Retribution and religious necessity mask the political machinations at work and functions well if you are David, the Gibeonites, or God. David gets rid of rival claimants to his throne, the Gibeonites are avenged of a perceived moral injury, and God is appeased. In other words, the sacrificial slaying of Saul's progeny provides the retributive justice that presumably reconciles David with the Gibeonites and with his God. Yet, it is difficult to reconcile the justice afforded to the Gibeonites, David, and God with a traumatized grieving Rizpah.

The king took the two sons of Rizpah daughter of Aiah, whom she bore to Saul, Armoni and Mephibosheth; and the five sons of Merab daughter of Saul, whom she bore to Adriel son of Barzillai the Meholathite; he gave them into the hands of the Gibeonites, and they impaled them on the mountain before the Lord. The seven of them perished together. They were put to death in the first days of harvest, at the beginning of barley harvest. Then

Rizpah the daughter of Aiah took sackcloth, and spread it on a rock for herself, from the beginning of harvest until rain fell on them from the heavens; she did not allow the birds of the air to come on the bodies by day, or the wild animals by night. (2 Samuel 21:8–10)

In the text, we find a complicated web of challenges that confront David and injure Rizpah. Her name appears only twice in the Old Testament. First, in 2 Samuel 3 where she is the subject of Ishbosheth's accusation against Abner of sexual assault. The accusation leads to Abner switching his allegiances from the house of Saul to the house of David. Although it is unclear whether Abner rapes Rizpah, the text gives voice to the vulnerability and tenuousness of her situation as a lower wife of a dead king. In 2 Samuel 21, as the secondary wife of the dethroned and deceased king Saul, Rizpah enters our purview as a widow whose two sons, together with five of Saul's grandsons, are slaughtered in what amounts to human sacrifice on the one hand and a sanctioned execution on the other. Thus, her story is disturbing not only for the unrestrained violence that it conveys but also for the unacknowledged traumatization of a woman who never utters a word in either of her limited appearances.

In writing on the anatomy of sociocultural oppression and the silencing of the oppressed, Kenneth Hardy writes, "Those who are dominated are not afforded the opportunity to discuss their condition or to negotiate with those who dominate."[6] As the widow of David's former rival, Rizpah belongs to a subjugated group. She is in the tenuous social position that many widows of the ancient world faced, where lacking male support made them vulnerable to various types of social injustices. Concern for the widow is the subject of many a prophetic critique. For example, Jeremiah 22:3 states,

> Thus says the Lord: execute judgment and righteousness and deliver the plundered out of the hand of the oppressor. Do no wrong and do no violence to the stranger, the fatherless, or the widow, nor shed innocent blood in this place.

Isaiah 1:17 admonishes, "Learn to do good; seek justice, rebuke the oppressor; defend the fatherless, plead for the widow."

Sadly, no one pleads for Rizpah, Merab, or their children. While the narrator includes the names of the mothers, curiously only the names of Rizpah's sons, Armoni and Mephibosheth are mentioned (2 Samuel 21:8). Perhaps Rizpah's sons were the last surviving members of her family and now they too were gone. As she has no connections to the Davidic house, she is alone and without support. Rizpah is powerless to prevent the king's men from entering her home and removing her sons. She watches as they are handed over to the Gibeonites. She has a front-row seat as the Gibeonites torture and impale them.[7] This mother witnesses their pain and hears their cries and shrieks of agony until life leaves their bodies. She watches as her sons are treated as enemies of the state and executed like criminals. Just like Emmett Till's uncle and cousins could not stop Roy Bryant and J. W. Milam from removing Emmett from their house, she could not stop David from taking her sons, could not stop the Gibeonites from killing them. So, she does what she can. The text says that she stands guard "from the beginning of the harvest till the rain poured down from the heavens on the bodies, she did not let the birds of the air touch them by day or the wild animals by night (2 Samuel 21:10)." Wilda Gafney paints a vivid portrait of Rizpah's vigil. "Rizpah bat Aiah watches the corpses of her sons stiffen, soften, swell, and sink into the stench of decay. . . . . . fights with winged, clawed, and toothed scavengers night and day. She is there from the spring harvest until the fall rains, as many as six months from Nissan (March/April) to Tishrei (September/October), sleeping, eating, toileting, protecting, and bearing witness."[8] There are no words to express her pain and grief—no words to express the injustice of what has been taken from her—no words to express the terror and horror of it all. We too are left speechless acknowledging our discomfort and the disturbing feelings the text arouses because violence, even when narrated, has a way of silencing the words of even the most responsive reader or interpreter.

The sons have been slaughtered and the shedding of blood that led to famine in the land has elicited more blood. Interestingly, the murder of these sons has not appeased God or ended the famine. Jonathan Magonet suggests Rizpah's actions represent "every mother who sees her sons killed before their time for reasons of state, be they in time of peace or in war. All that remains is for her to preserve the dignity of their memory and live on to bear witness and call to account the rulers of the world."[9] In the wake of senseless violence, these mothers relive the deaths of their sons as traumatic memories that continually interrupt the present. Their waking moments are haunted by these memories and their nights riddled with *what if*. Amy Beth Jones and Stephanie Day Powell intimate such a *what if* in their Mishradic reading of Rizpah's vigil in which they seek to "bring to the surface the displaced grief of mothers who lose their sons to institutional forms of violence."[10]

Rizpah's silent vigil over the dead bodies of these sons is evidence of her grief and becomes the visible bodily response to the traumatic conditions attending their deaths and her powerlessness to stop it. As a mother, she will remember her birth pains together with the piercing cries that accompanied their deaths and every day she spent with them in between. For her (and perhaps for us), it is not enough that the exposed unburied bodies of the slain violated Israel's burial practices where the dead received a prompt burial out of respect (Deuteronomy 21:23). There are also the power dynamics that placed her sons at the mercy of the king in the first place. Again, Boesak's comments are instructive, he states, "As she fights against the beasts of the field, she fights at the same time against the beasts in the palace—those men who rule, who have decided they have power, like God, over the lives and the deaths of these young men."[11] Rizpah is subordinate to the coercive and abusive control that the king exerts over the lives and bodies of his subjects. For her, the matter of reconciliation and justice remains elusive not simply because traumatic experiences harbor lingering wounds but also because she is unable to confront the king directly and exact the justice that the deaths of her sons demanded.

For this reason, Rizpah's vigil exposes why reconciliation can be an uncomfortable, contested space that exposes inequitable distributions of power. Reconciliation assumes that parity exists between two parties. David represents the monarchy and the power that comes with it. Men go into battle at his command and women are taken for his personal pleasure (2 Samuel 11). David is not moved to have the bodies of Saul and Jonathan buried when they are slain and put on display by the Philistines on Mount Gilboa in 1 Samuel 31. This is striking given his public display of mourning the two men upon hearing of their deaths (2 Samuel 1:11–13). Neither is he moved to bury Saul's recently executed sons and grandsons, as the text makes no mention of his attempt to secure their bodies prior to hearing about Rizpah's vigil. He determines the rules of social and political engagement with others. Given the lack of parity, he cannot define the terms of reconciliation nor actualize it for those subjugated under his rule since to do so would amount to further abuse of his power.[12] David's access to privilege and the power he wields stand in stark contrast to the powerlessness of Rizpah. Like Mamie Till-Mobley, everyone could see what they had done to her boys.

Rizpah's vigil is both a lament and remembrance that shames perhaps bringing public opinion as her recourse. She may occupy a position of marginalization, but her truth (and the justice it demands) shames the most powerful person of her day, King David, to act on behalf of the dead (2 Samuel 21:11). Gafney summarizes the point well: "lynching Rizpah's and Merab's sons did not heal the land or the people. Doing right by the multiple wronged woman did."[13] Indeed, the text states that it is only after David retrieves and buries the remains of the slain that "God heeded supplications for the land" (2 Samuel 21:14).[14] Is it possible to conceptualize Rizpah's act as one that results in a small token of restorative justice? Such an understanding makes it possible to view her vigil as an act of resistance where restoration is a feasible outcome. Yet, in this narrative, it is important that we ask who and what is being restored? By forcing the king through his conscience to decide, discuss, detoxify, and devote energy to retrieving the dead, Rizpah's actions restore the king and his honor.[15] While she may have the satisfaction and closure of seeing her sons and those of Merab's buried, her grief and the trauma of their deaths remain an open wound. She does not interact or reconcile with David nor do we hear that his actions evoked a sense of forgiveness on her part. The story concludes simply with "after that God heeded supplications for the land" (2 Samuel 21:14), which points back to David's initial concern over the famine. Still, Rizpah's vigil must not be interpreted solely as an act of a peaceful warrior who operates with a heart of peace and a spirit of war.[16] She must not be classified or categorized as a nonviolent resister to the evil of the situation. We interpret Rizpah's silent vigil as a counter-cultural response that challenges normative understandings of reconciliation as unambiguous spaces of comfort, but instead as contested, uncomfortable spaces that expose and confront inequitable distributions of power. Her story is a wake-up call for those of us in theological education and the church to engage in the redemptive work that addresses the realities of traumatic suffering and helps people give meaning to their traumatic experiences.

Reconciliation and Restorative Justice

Reconciliation can refer to either a process or an intended outcome. Stanford's *Encyclopedia of Philosophy* defines reconciliation as

> An outcome . . . an improvement in the relations among parties formerly at odds with one another . . . Two parties will count as reconciled only if their better future relations result from their having satisfactorily dealt with the emotional, epistemic, and/or material legacy of the past. While the future outcome of reconciliation is oriented

> toward a future marked by peaceful and just relations, the processes of reconciliation are typically oriented towards the continuing bad feelings, suspicions, or harms created by the conflicts and injustices of the past.[17]

Reconciliation is oftentimes linked with the concept of forgiveness. While these concepts are often used synonymously, Robert Enright distinguishes between the two. He submits, "to forgive is to know that you have been treated unjustly and, despite the injustice, make the decision to reduce your resentment toward the offending person and eventually work toward mercy. That mercy can take the form of kindness, respect, generosity, and even love."[18] For Enright, reconciliation is "the process of two or more people coming together in mutual trust (with an emphasis on the word mutual) after a process of forgiving and seeking forgiveness. Without mutual trust, reconciliation is not possible."[19] In contrast, Boesak examines the issue in terms of risk and resistance and concludes that Rizpah's action is "an intrusion, a disturbance, an uncomfortable presence deliberately brought into the cycle of triumphant David-stories."[20]

Frequently subsumed under the theme of forgiveness, reconciliation in the Bible seeks to address moral and ethical issues that arise in human interactions (i.e., friendships, family, nation, etc.). For example, Matthew 5:23–24 states, "Therefore if you are offering your gift at the altar and there remember that your brother or sister has something against you, leave your gift there before the altar. First, go and be reconciled to your brother or sister and then come and offer your gift." In Genesis 33, Jacob is reconciled to his estranged brother Esau many years after a stew dinner leaves Esau bereft of a birthright. Elsewhere in Genesis 50, we find the reconciliation of Joseph to his brothers, who, having sold him into slavery, seek his forgiveness and goodwill. Joseph's utterance in 50:20 marks their future relationship, "Even though you intended to do harm to me, God intended it for good, in order to preserve a numerous people, as God is doing today."

These examples suggest that the issue of justice, as it pertains to reconciliation, is undermined in the pursuit of peace and that people must choose between one or the other. However, the words of Martin Luther King Jr. are a poignant reminder that the matter is not either/or, but both/and, when he writes, "true peace is not merely the absence of tension: it is the presence of justice."[21] There can be no reconciliation without justice, no justice without truth, and no truth without love, an admonishment that reverberates throughout 2 Samuel 21:1–14. In the words of Cornel West, "Justice is what love looks like in public, just like tenderness is what love feels like in private."[22] Here, we do not attempt an exhaustive treatment of the topics retributive justice (punishment) and restorative justice (correcting imbalances). Yet, holding persons accountable for acts of injustice would seemingly go a long way in promoting reconciliation. Or does it? Unfortunately, this is not the case for Rizpah; the texts cited above offer a perception that looks to the reconciliation of individuals and families with no overt attention to matters of justice. When reading 2 Samuel 21:1–14, context and perspective matter. We offer that this narrative is not a good example of reconciliation nor is it a good example of restorative justice when read through the lens of trauma.

Trauma and Grief as a Pastoral Care Concern

Unmistakably, the story's narration of the Gibeonites' execution of the seven sons of Saul is violent in its presentation and violent in its proclamation. Under the guise of reconciliation and retributive justice, the reader is astonished by the callous abuse of power and the manipulation of religious symbolism that pejoratively reflect on David, the Gibeonites, and God. Yet, Rizpah's actions as a grieving mother interrupt and disrupt the violent nature of the narrative. Further, she contains and compartmentalizes her grief and trauma in a manner that allows her to effectively respond to the abuse of power and the minimization and marginalization of her humanity. In a modern context, Rizpah's silent vigil resonates with the cry for justice by countless mothers and family members who have watched their children and relatives sacrificed to state-sanctioned brutality, and the political and socio-economic exigencies of our society (i.e., George Floyd, Eric Garner, Trayvon Martin, Tyree Nichols, and others).[23] Phillip Goff commented to the *Huffington Post*, "the perception that the perpetrators of violence face no consequences can transform that trauma into terror."[24] Trauma and terror inform the existential realities for most oppressed individuals and groups, who understand that reconciliation serves to appease the conscience of the oppressor rather than ensure justice for the oppressed.

As a trauma survivor, Rizpah is one of the walking wounded. Trauma survivors struggle with and harbor wounds that persist over time and situations. In his seminal work, *The Body Keeps the Score: Brain, Mind, and Body in the Healing of Trauma*, Bessel van der Kolk writes,

> As human beings we belong to an extremely resilient species. Since time immemorial we have rebounded from our relentless wars, countless disasters (both natural and man-made), and the violence and betrayal in our own lives. But traumatic experiences do leave traces, whether on a large scale (on our histories and cultures) or close to home, on our families, with dark secrets being imperceptibly passed down through generations. They also leave traces on our minds and emotions, on our capacity for joy and intimacy, and even on our biology and immune systems.[25]

The effects of trauma manifest not only in those who experience a traumatic event but also in those who witness it. Carrie Doehring describes trauma as a "bio-psycho-spiritual response to overwhelming life events that like earthquakes open up crevasses deep down into core belief, values, and ways of coping. It is an existential crisis or de-centering experience that disrupts the world as one knows it."[26] These experiences have been shown to result in life-long attachment-emotional challenges described as "injuries to heart and soul," where bruised hearts, hardened hearts, addicted hearts, and over-functioning over-performing hearts are cataclysmic and can lead to other mental health issues.[27]

Similarly, Shelly Rambo explains trauma as "an encounter with death. This encounter is not, however, a literal death but a way of describing a radical event or events that shatter all that one knows about the world and all the familiar ways of operating within it."[28] Laurie Pearlman explicitly describes traumatic death as a sudden, abrupt loss of life, writing:

> Although lack of anticipation alone can render a death traumatizing to a survivor, a death is more likely to be traumatic if it is untimely; if it involves violence or mutilation; if the survivor regards it as preventable; if the survivor believes that the loved one suffered; or if the survivor regards the death, or manner of death, as unfair and unjust. Other kinds of deaths likely to be regarded as traumatic include a death perceived as random (i.e., the loved one was in the wrong place at the wrong time); a death caused by a perpetrator with intent to harm; a situation where the survivor witnessed the death; a situation where the survivor is confronted with many deaths; and situations where the survivor's own life is threatened.[29]

Trauma hijacks one's emotions and perception of the world, affecting how one operates within it. Some of the lingering effects that plague the traumatized include repression and silence, sensations (panic attacks) and images, or the outward manifestation of rage, anger, and shame. Unacknowledged or repression of traumatic memories do not alleviate the pain and suffering of the traumatized and frequently leads them to harm themselves or others. Some (not all) experiences of complicated trauma and grief result in a person experiencing long term bouts with Post Traumatic Stress Disorder (PTSD). Moreover, it is not uncommon for the traumatized to undergo a crisis of faith where the spiritual seems meaningless in a world that now is perceived as hostile and distrustful (even God has abandoned them).

Still, discussions on trauma must be understood in tandem with discussions on grief, specifically traumatic grief. Grief is a normal response to any significant or meaningful loss (anticipated or unanticipated). For example, one experiences grief at the death of a loved one to cancer or another chronic illness. The person grieving can expect to go through various stages of mental suffering (denial, anger, bargaining, depression, and acceptance).[30] The experience of grief allows the person to heal over time. Paul Rosenblatt and Beverly Wallace contend that while grief is a universal experience, for African Americans, it is nuanced by racism. They proffer "in order to understand African American grief it is important to understand how an African American death may have been caused in whole or in part by racism."[31] How else might one justify or account for the deaths of Michael Brown in Ferguson, Missouri; Eric Garner in New York City; Tamir Rice in Cleveland, Ohio; Philando Castile in St. Paul, Minnesota; Freddie Gray in Baltimore, Maryland; George Floyd in Minneapolis, Minnesota; Trevon Martin in Sanford, Florida; and Tyree Nichols in Memphis, Tennessee, and the list goes on and on. All these young Black males, some Black mother's son, died or were murdered by the very people who pledged an oath of office to protect. Indeed, this is traumatic grief, or what pastoral psychologist Melissa Kelley calls grief born of injustice. She states, "By grief born of injustice, I mean the following: it is grief due in whole or in part to injustice. It is grief that is caused by unjust structures and/or by unjust actions or inactions of individuals, groups, and systems."[32] Traumatic grief is more profound and more intense, and therefore more complicated than normal grief. The traumatic event interrupts the normal process of healing that accompanies grief. The ability to remember and come to terms with the death of a loved one is not possible as those memories are intertwined with the images of the traumatic event that caused the loved one's death. Pearlman submits, "When a person has suffered a traumatic loss, attempts to recollect the loved one are often associated with distressing memories or images, such as what happened during the loved one's death. These thoughts and images are so disturbing that in many cases, individuals try to avoid thinking about their loved one, making it far more difficult to process their loss."[33]

We have emphasized the complicated effects of trauma and grief on survivors. However, what of those who become witnesses to another's suffering? How do pastors and congregations come alongside the traumatized and ensure that they *do no harm* as they themselves become emotionally vulnerable when hearing the stories of traumatized persons or witnessing the outward manifestations of traumatic grief and its lingering effects?

Responses to Traumatic Grief

Due to the traumatic impacts of racism and discrimination, African Americans find themselves in need of pastoral care interventions at the individual and communal levels. One of the traditional functions of pastoral care is the healing of the soul. What kind of pastoral interventions or rituals can promote healing within Black families and Black communities when family members, friends, or congregants experience traumatic grief as the result of a traumatic death? We offer a trifold therapeutic response to addressing this question: the funeral, counseling, and advocacy in the form of social protest.

Funerals

The Bible contains several stories that depict how ancient communities showed honor and respect for the dead (e.g., Genesis 23; Genesis 50:1–14; 1 Samuel 31:11–12). These rituals are culturally embedded in Israelite society. For a vast majority in the African American community, the funeral is a resource to address their grief and is a significant ritual in honoring their dead. In reference to Black funerals, African American pastoral theologian Chanequa Walker-Barnes submits,

> Dying and mourning have always been serious business among people of African descent. The sacredness attached to death and funerals is a remnant of African cultures that survived the trans-Atlantic slave trade, European

> colonization, and cultural assimilation. Thus, West African traditions of honoring family and the deceased with elaborate memorials and visitation continue to be important rituals among Blacks in the United States.[34]

In the African American community within the Christian context, the funeral often is identified as a "Celebration of Life," "Homegoing," or "Homecoming" service, and rituals surrounding it serve as a means of memorializing and validating the worth of the dead. It speaks to the fact that the deceased was loved and cared for by a community consisting of biological and adopted family members, near and far relatives, a host of friends and associates. The Homegoing service is a mixture of sadness but also a celebration of the life of the individual who upon their death returns to God. Conceivably, the community provides the deceased's last testament, an indication that she/he was born, lived, and loved.

Exquisite detail is given to the funeral's composition so that it reflects the uniqueness of the deceased. The service is preceded by a time of visitation or wake in which family are greeted by those who knew their dearly departed loved one. Here emotional support is expressed through touch (hugs), words, cards, and monetary gifts. In her work, *Passed On: African American Mourning Stories*, Karla Holliday acknowledges the significance of the wake among African Americans. She states, "in the particular communities of African Americans, the wake is the appropriate first occasion to extend comfort and assistance to the bereaved family."[35] Upon conclusion of the wake, the funeral service begins immediately with the procession of clergy, the citing of scripture about the fragility of life, a prayer of consolation, gospel songs, and hymns. Words of encouragement by clergy, memories shared by family members and friends, and the reading of sympathy cards and resolutions followed by a eulogy that seeks to place the life of the deceased within an eternal context of meaning all attend a service that can be short and brief or expand several hours.

The final act is the graveside committal followed by the repast. The repast is a time in which family and friends gather to share a meal. From their qualitative study of the African American funeral, Rosenblatt and Wallace assert,

> What was mentioned most often was the food, which was brought to feed those who were grieving and to relieve them from responsibilities for preparing food . . . food seemed an essential part of post funeral gatherings of family, friends, and community members. At one level, the food is about something like communion. At another level, it is a way to assure that people who are preoccupied with their grief or who have come from far away have something to eat.[36]

Rosenblatt and Wallace note the exquisite attention given to funeral rituals. "African Americans may put relatively great resources of money and time into providing the proper funeral and into attending funerals . . . Perhaps an important aspect of such a heavy investment in funerals is that as Barrett wrote, 'African American funerals . . . represent a posthumous attempt for dignity and esteem denied and limited by the dominant culture.'"[37] In sum, the funeral with its pageantry and performance provides a safe space.[38] These expressions of grief can be a cathartic release that is therapeutic.

Trauma Informed Counseling

Another resource by which healing can take place is through trauma-informed pastoral care interventions. Trauma-informed pastoral care seeks to avoid reinjury and promote healing. Karen McClintock, using a government model, offers what she refers to as the four "Rs" of trauma-informed care:

> Realize trauma's impact on individuals and groups
>
> Recognize the signs and symptoms of trauma
>
> Respond to trauma with supportive services
>
> Resist retraumatization by creating safe, supportive, and collaborative partnerships with survivors.[39]

However, she includes a fifth "R": that of reconnecting. The trauma survivor's pain and injury can only be alleviated with support and intervention. If trauma disconnects the survivor by disrupting the person's world where trust, bonds, and faith have been shattered, reconnecting becomes a crucial element in the healing process. Grief and trauma must be conceptualized as invitations to interventions and not monsters of the mind. This is especially true when the survivors are among the most vulnerable and the least resourced in our society. From a pastoral care perspective, the concern is mitigating the ongoing suffering of the traumatized. Christian theology often approaches the topic of suffering through the classic framework of theodicy; however, we suggest the need to "witness to," intervene with, and focus on the experiences of the sufferer by creating safe, non-judgmental spaces that allow them to tell their stories of traumatization. To abide with the traumatized in the most uncomfortable of spaces, providing the ministry of presence where there are no right answers and there are no simple fixes is the work of the shepherd, the work of pastoral care, in essence, the work of the Church. Moreover, even if our Rizpahs are not restored or reconciled, they must still be loved and cared for! We must hold the abused and traumatized survivors in love and action, in interventions where the church rallies and responds. Still, the church does not do this work alone. Clinical psychologists and pastoral psychotherapists specializing in spirituality, family trauma, and mental health must also be engaged so that the Rizpahs of this contemporary age can rebuild their lives in a manner that restores hope, compassion, and agency. In this process of therapeutic rebuilding, a combination of family system therapy, dialectical behavioral therapy, and restorative justice-based social intervention can be very fruitful.

Advocacy as Social Protest

A third resource that has been employed by African Americans in dealing with their grief is social protest. Historically, African

Americans have employed social protest through various means to express their outrage and unfavorable sentiment on social injustices perpetrated upon them by the dominant power structure. Their response to these social injustices has consisted of marches where African Americans and their sympathizers have banded together to "parade" through the streets as a unified group to demonstrate their discontent with an unjust social policy, heinous event, or inhuman treatment. Two significant marches that stand out in the history of America are the Harlem Silent Parade in 1917, which sought to address the violence perpetrated upon African Americans in New York, and the Selma to Montgomery marches, which advocated for voter rights for African Americans in Alabama.

Another form of social protest have been rallies, where African Americans gather at a particular location to hear speakers address social injustices and vociferously offer a critique of the white power structure that supports it. A most famous example of this type of social protest was the March on Washington in 1963, which advocated for jobs and economic opportunities for African Americans. A third form of social protest have been pickets and sit-ins, where African Americans surround, occupy, or block off strategic areas seeking to bring public attention to a specific social injustice. Memorable examples of this type of social protest are the Greensboro sit-ins during the Civil Rights Movement in 1960s in Greensboro, North Carolina and the 1968 Memphis sanitation strike, when sanitations workers carrying picket signs that read "I am a man" went on strike to challenge the power structure for fair wages and improved environmental conditions.

A more contemporary social protest movement against violence against the African American community is the Black Lives Matter Movement. According to Derald Wing Sue et al., "The African American community has consistently named police violence directed at their communities as a social problem and demanded justice and reform. The Movement for Black Lives reflects the most recent efforts."[40] Each of these movements provided African Americans with a vehicle to express their moral indignation, objection, and outrage related to social injustices or acts perpetrated upon individuals in their community. The intent of social protest is to bring attention to the concern and influence public opinion. Although it has been a means of nonviolent civil disobedience, it has often erupted into violence and loss of life. These three interventions—the funeral, formal trauma informed counseling and social protest—have been ways in which traumatic grief has been addressed to bring about healing within the lived experience of African Americans and the Black community.

Conclusion

An uncritical reading of 2 Samuel 21 might tempt us to glorify King David for stepping into a difficult situation and "making it better." We might even read its sacrificial tenor and tone as a reflection of the social and religious climate in which it was produced, the creation of a community in crisis. At the same time, we must not overlook the psychological, social, spiritual, and traumatic elements that are interlaced within the narrative to the detriment of the women (and sons), who function as narrative foils. Rizpah performs a long grueling vigil (Gafney) and conducts a memorial ceremony (Magonet). For Rizpah, the elements of trauma are easily identified as she responds to an overwhelming life event (Doehring) and reconciles her psyche with the fact that her sons are dead (Rambo). These psycho-social stressors most likely exacerbated her feelings of grief and suffering, thus compounding the trauma she possibly felt. Yes, Rizpah's vigil is powerful, but it is not redemptive, nor is it restorative, and when viewed in those terms it is unreconcilable. One could argue whether David does right by Rizpah. Her sons receive a proper burial, but the decision that cost them their lives (which we interpret as an unjust act) remains in the realm of the privileged and powerful. Rizpah, like Mamie Till-Mobley and the African American women whose children have died due to the excessive force of some police officers who abused their positions of authority, found a way in her silence to give voice to her grief and suffering.[41]

The pastoral implications are clear. While there is no resurrection of Rizpah's sons, current-day Rizpahs can be ministered to in the shadow of the cross. Here, we offer that those traumatized do not need church or biblical platitudes. Rather, they need a healing discourse that allows them to bear witness to their experience such that they are able to move beyond it, despite its lingering effects upon the psyche. If trauma is the "storm that does not go away," as Rambo suggests, then the church must be prepared to serve as lifeboats of redemption rooted in the Spirit and love of Christ.

Discussion Questions

- How can silence become a mechanism to promote healing?
- Discuss the significance of "being with" or "abiding with" a person during moments of tragedy.
- What image of God is depicted in this story? Does this portrait of God make you comfortable or uncomfortable? Why?
- How do you respond to the statement that "Rizpah's vigil is powerful, but not redemptive"?

Additional Resources:

Bruce C. Birch et al., *The New Interpreter's Bible: Numbers–Samuel* (Abingdon Press, 1998).

Danielle J. Buhuro, *Spiritual Care in an Age of #BLACKLIVES-MATTER* (Cascade Books, 2019).

Robert Enright, *Forgiveness Is a Choice: A Step-by-Step Process for Resolving Anger and Restoring Hope* (American Psychological Association, 2019).

Cephas T. A. Tushima, *The Fate of Saul's Progeny in the Reign of David* (The Lutterworth Press, 2011).

Endnotes

1 Elliot J. Gorn, *Let the People See: The Story of Emmett Till* (Oxford University Press, 2018), 1.

2 Tony Cartledge offers that it is Saul's violation of an oath that led to the blood guilt upon his house. The violation was enough to provoke the Israelite deity's anger and the subsequent plague as punishment for the violation. See Tony W. Cartledge, *1 & 2 Samuel* (Smyth & Helwys Publishing, 2001), 638.

3 J. Cheryl Exum, "Rizpah," *Word & World* 17, no. 3 (1997): 264.

4 Allan Aubrey Boesak, "Reconciliation, Risk, and Resistance: The Story of Rizpah," in *Radical Reconciliation: Beyond Political Pietism and Christian Quietism* (Orbis Books, 2012), 30.

5 Walter Brueggemann, *First and Second Samuel* (Westminster John Knox Press, 2012), 337.

6 Kenneth V. Hardy, "Toward a Psychology of the Oppressed: Understanding the Invisible Wounds of Trauma," in *Re-Visioning Family Therapy: Addressing Diversity in Clinical Practice*, ed. Monica McGoldrick and Kenneth V. Hardy (Guilford Publications, 2019), 136.

7 The text is unclear on exactly how the sons and grandsons met their deaths: "Ritual dismemberment seems likely, though hanging, impalement, crucifixion, being broken on the wheel, or cast down from a height have all been suggested." Exum, "Rizpah," 263.

8 Wilda C. Gafney, *Womanist Midrash: A Reintroduction to the Women of the Torah and the Throne* (Westminster John Knox Press, 2017), 200, 201.

9 Jonathan Magonet, *Bible Lives* (SCM Press, 1992), 11.

10 Amy Beth Jones and Stephanie Day Powell, "Rizpah's Vigil: A Midrash on Grief (2 Samuel 21:1–14)," in *Bridging the Divide Between Bible and Practical Theology*, ed. Denise Hopkins and Michael Koppel (Cambridge Publishing, 2018), 137–144.

11 Boesak, "Reconciliation, Risk, and Resistance," 31.

12 Ibid., 37.

13 Gafney, *Womanist Midrash*, 201.

14 Ibid.

15 Clinical psychologist Everette Worthington discusses the difference between forgiveness and reconciliation in which the bridge to reconciliation requires an intentional pathway that involves

decision making, discussion, detoxification and devotion. For a fuller discussion of Worthington's concepts see chapters 9-12 in Everett Worthington, *Forgiving and Reconciling: Bridges to Wholeness and Hope* (InterVarsity Press, 2003).

16 The concept of the peaceful warrior is based on the graphic novel by Dan Millman, *Way of the Peaceful Warrior: A Book That Changes Lives* (H J Kramer, 2006).

17 Linda Radzik and Colleen Murphy, "Reconciliation," *Stanford Encyclopedia of Philosophy*, ed. Edward N. Zalta, August 2, 2019, https://plato.stanford.edu/entries/reconciliation.

18 Robert Enright, *The Forgiving Life: A Pathway to Overcoming Resentment and Creating a Legacy of Love* (American Psychological Association, 2012), 26–27.

19 Ibid., 106.

20 Boesak, "Reconciliation, Risk, and Resistance," 25.

21 Martin Luther King Jr., "Letter from Birmingham Jail," https://letterfromjail.com/.

22 Cornel West, "Askwith Forum," virtual lecture, October 4, 2017, by Harvard Graduate School of Education, YouTube, 1:36:19, https://youtu.be/zuxqhsrCGeg.

23 Women who have also been victims of state-sponsored killings include Alberta Spruill, Rekia Boyd, Shantel Davis, Shelly Frey, Kayla Moore, Kyam Livingston, Miriam Carey, Michelle Cusseaux, Tanisha Anderson, and others. See "About #SayHerName," African American Policy Forum, https://www.aapf.org/sayhername.

24 Liz Adetiba and Anna Almendrala, "Watching Videos of Police Brutality Can Traumatize You, Especially If You're Black," *Huffington Post*, July 8, 2016, https://www.huffpost.com/entry/watching-police-brutality-videos_n_577ee9b3e4b0344d514eaa5d.

25 Bessel van der Kolk, *The Body Keeps the Score: Brain, Mind, and Body in the Healing of Trauma* (Viking, 2014), 1.

26 Carrie Doehring, "Spiritual Care After Violence: Growing from Trauma with Lived-Theology," Biola University Center for Christian Thought, June 23, 2014, https://cct.biola.edu/spiritual-care-violence-growing-trauma-lived-theology/.

27 Tim Clinton and Gary Sibcy, *Attachments: Why You Love, Feel, and Act the Way You Do* (Integrity Publishing, 2002).

28 Shelly Rambo, *Spirit and Trauma: A Theology of Remaining* (Westminster John Knox Press, 2010), 3.

29 Laurie Anne Pearlman et al., *Treating Traumatic Bereavement: A Practitioner's Guide* (The Guilford Press, 2014), 4.

30 Elisabeth Kübler-Ross, *On Death and Dying: What the Dying Have to Teach Doctors, Nurses, Clergy and Their Families* (Scribner Publishing Company, 2014), 37–132.

31 Paul C. Rosenblatt and Beverly R. Wallace, *African American Grief* (Routledge Press, 2005), 7.

32 Melissa Kelley, *Grief: Contemporary Theory and the Practice of Ministry* (Fortress Press, 2010), 15.

33 Pearlman et al., *Treating Traumatic Bereavement*, 6.

34 Chanequa Walker-Barnes, *Too Heavy a Yoke: Black Women and the Burden of Strength* (Cascade Books, 2014), vi–vii.

35 Karla FC Holloway, *Passed On: African American Mourning Stories* (North Carolina University Press, 2003), 165.

36 Rosenblatt and Wallace, *African American Grief*, 31.

37 Ibid., 29.

38 Ibid., 39.

39 Karen A. McClintock, *Trauma-Informed Pastoral Care: How to Respond When Things Fall Apart* (Fortress Press, 2022), 16. McClintock's model is derived from one developed for a governmental agency.

40 Derald Wing Sue et al., *Counseling the Culturally Diverse: Theory and Practice*, 9th ed. (Wiley Press, 2022), 225.

41 Michael Sebastian, "Who Are the 'Mothers of the Movement' Speaking at the Democratic National Convention?," *ELLE*, July 26, 2016, https://www.elle.com/culture/career-politics/news/a38111/who-are-mothers-of-the-movement-dnc/.

4

Restoring the Fathers, Saving Our Sons: An Empathetic Reading of Jephthah's Vow in Judges 11:30–31

Raynard D. Smith

The narrative of Jephthah the Gileadite offers a lens to examine the lived experience of many African American males who grow up in matrifocal homes where the father is absent, whether emotionally or physically.[1] This examination suggests that as a lived experience, fatherlessness leaves Black males with a pervasive longing for their biological father. This absence may cause social dislocation and loss of identity, particularly within a society that idealizes the nuclear family.[2] A re-reading of Jephthah's story allows us to explore the issue of fatherlessness and its implications for a contemporary audience, namely, Black Churches, while offering a pastoral care intervention that encompasses grief work and forgiveness.

Studies suggest that African American males who grow up in fatherless homes suffer in silence, harboring negative feelings about themselves and their desired fathers.[3] When suppressed, these feelings may result in behaviors that manifest as poor decisions throughout their lives. Frequently, poor choices driven or motivated by unconscious and conscious feelings of anger, resentment, betrayal, or ambivalence (love and hate) require an intervention that addresses these feelings. This, in turn, might lead to healing and wholeness (moving from immature manhood to mature manhood). This healing consists of three phases: 1) mourning—the need to grieve the absence of the father (physically or emotionally) and thereby let go of the conscious or unconscious desire for his presence, 2) forgiveness—the need to forgive the guilty desired father for the absence of his presence, and 3) mentoring—the need to establish new and reliable relationships with a mature older Black male. To accomplish this work of healing calls for Black Churches to become aware that Black males growing up fatherless need emotional, psychological, and spiritual support to help heal the unacknowledged injury that fatherlessness engenders.

Israel's God Drama

The book of Judges depicts the ambiguity and complexity of covenantal loyalty. The story of Jephthah takes place within the larger historical drama of Israel's relationship with its God, Yahweh. Israel has difficulty adhering to the deity's directive to "have no other gods before me" (Exodus 20:3). The constant failure to comply with the covenant results in a cycle of apostasy that requires the intervention of judges. The term "judge" as it appears in both the book's title and as a descriptor for the book's main characters has only minor affinities with our contemporary understanding of the word. In the biblical text, the word refers to governing over, ruling, and/or leading armies. The term is best understood when viewed as a series of acts of governance rather than unique acts of condemnation. Thus, judges are those who either "save" and/or "judge" Israel and fall within two categories: charismatic leaders and institutional administrators. In the case of charismatic leaders, the spirit of Yahweh empowers the leader to perform supernatural feats of strength, power, and wisdom, which enables them to defeat the enemies of Israel during times of war (see Judges 3:10, 6:34, 11:29, and 14:6). Institutional administrators serve as judges during periods of peace (see Judges10:1-2, 3-5; 12:11, 13–15). The book depicts the cyclical pattern of apostasy, judgment, outcry, Yahweh's intervention via a judge, a time of peace or rest, death of the judge, and the return to apostasy.

In times before when Israel remembered their covenantal relationship with Yahweh, put away their idols in repentance, and sought Yahweh's forgiveness, their pleas were met favorably with God's compassion and forgiveness. Yahweh then avenged them of their enemies. However, this time when Israel confesses their sins in Judges 10:10, Yahweh refuses to hear and acknowledge their change of heart. "Did I not deliver you . . . Yet you have abandoned me and worshipped other gods; therefore, I will deliver you no more. Go and cry to the gods whom you have chosen; let them deliver you in the time of your distress" (Judges 10:11–14). According to Barry Webb,

> Yahweh recognizes the purely utilitarian nature of their cry and confronts them with it. Israel cries to Yahweh rather than to others because they judge him to be more useful to them in their present circumstance (your time of trouble). He speaks as one who knows that he has been used in this way in the past (12b-13b) and is determined not be used again. That is though the cry here has the accoutrements of repentance, it is not accepted at its face value by Yahweh.[4]

The Israelites continued idolatry draws the deity's ire resulting in the advancement of their enemies and the ultimate breakdown of their defenses (Judges 10:6–9). Yahweh emphatically refuses to let them get away with their empty promises to clean up their act. But again, even though Yahweh refused to act immediately on their behalf, their cries and groans are overwhelming, touching Yahweh's heart of compassion. Although Yahweh's frustration with Israel is evident, the deity can no longer bear to see Israel suffer (10:16b). But has Yahweh truly forgiven them in a manner that holds Israel accountable for their covenantal infidelity? The stage is set as the Ammonites advance to Gilead for war against the Israelites (10:17–18). While in Mizpah, the leaderless Israelites prepare to defend themselves against the anticipated Ammonite invasion. The uncertainty of Yahweh's intervention on Israel's behalf comes across as a textual silence as the reader awaits the deity's decision. Will Yahweh intervene on their behalf and once again send a deliverer?

The Family Saga of Jephthah

There is a saying that "desperate times call for desperate measures." The Israelites are desperate! Unable to find a volunteer to lead their army, Jephthah the Gileadite enters the narrative. Although a "mighty warrior," Jephthah is the son of a prostitute, a *zonah* (זנה), and his father "Gilead" may have been any one of the men from Gilead (Judges 11:1).[5] The Hebrew *zonah*, according to Kimberly Russaw, "points to a woman who exists on the margins of acceptable society because she participates in sex work."[6] As a prostitute, Jephthah's mother is a stigmatized member of the Israelite society, both in urban and rural life (Genesis 38:14; Joshua 2:1ff.; 1 Kings 3:16–27).[7] Here, Wilda Gafney's notion of the sanctified imagination can be instructive to our exploration of the gaps that exist in Jephthah's narrative. She describes the sanctified imagination as "the fertile space where the preacher-interpreter enters the text, particularly the spaces in the text, and fills them out with missing details, names, back stories, detailed descriptions of the scene and characters, and so on."[8] As one who grew up in the Black Church where I witnessed this creative style of preaching and having utilized it with my own preaching, I come to the story of Jephthah with this same devotion in mind. For me it is a form of disciplined subjectivity that seeks to be faithful to scripture while also employing psychological insights.

While the text does not state that Jephthah lived with his mother, who participated in a dishonorable profession in order to maintain her household, the textual lacuna lends itself to this possibility.[9] Russaw's conclusions suggest as much. She submits, "By identifying his mother's profession as that of a sex worker and suggesting his father was an indistinguishable Gileadite, the writer introduces tension in the story from the beginning . . . His problematic parentage does not position Jephthah as a candidate for leadership."[10] The text states that Jephthah flees his home when his half-brothers reject him, "You shall not inherit anything in our father's house for you are the son of another mother" (Judges 11:2b). Spurned, alienated, rejected, and disinherited by his half-brothers, Jephthah gathers around himself a gang of outlaws and engages in criminal activity in Tob to sustain himself (11:2–3). As the leader of these mercenaries, an alternate family structure to be sure, Jephthah establishes himself as quite a consummate warrior. This ill-gained notoriety leads the Israelite elders to request that Jephthah take charge of Israel's military defense against the Ammonites.

Those who ousted him now stand in need of his military skills (Judges 11:5–7). They entice him with the promise to make him "head over all the inhabitants of Gilead" (11:8). Is it possible that the Israelites' need for a champion meets Jephthah's need to belong?[11] Speculatively, do the elders think him so naive or vain that he would unquestionably assume command of their army? Furthermore, would accepting their offer reunite him with his community, bring him honor, and satisfy his need for a positive identity to belong? How we are brought to this shift, the text does not say. What it does reveal is that the Israelites' need for military leadership outweighs Jephthah's status as a criminal and social outcast. However, like Yahweh before, Jephthah expresses his apprehension in responding immediately to their request. He retorts, "Are you not the very ones who rejected me and drove me out of my father's house? So why do you come to me now when you are in trouble?" (11:7). Their response fails to acknowledge his question but rather reiterates their desperation, "We have now turned back to you, so that you may go with us and fight with the Ammonites, and become head over us, over all the inhabitants of Gilead (11:8)." Without any sense of remorse, the elders make a counteroffer that would make Jephthah their tribal chief. Jephthah, the son of a prostitute, ascends to a position of notoriety from the obscurity of the underclass. His acceptance of their offer reveals that he, too, is desperate. He says to the elders, "If you bring me home again to fight with the Ammonites, and the Lord gives them over to me, I will be your head" (11:9).

Jephthah's two failed attempts for a peaceful resolution with the Ammonites result in his seeking a divine solution. Yet, he still requires confirmation and assurance of his victory despite having the spirit of his god (Yahweh) come upon him. With his self-confidence waning and his all-pervasive desire to be accepted still unsatisfied, Jephthah strikes a bargain with Yahweh and vows, "If you will give me the Ammonites into my hand, then whoever comes out of the doors of my house to meet me, when I return victoriously from the Ammonites, shall be the Lord's, to be offered up by me as a burnt offering (11:30–31)."[12] He defeats the Ammonites and now must return home to make good on his vow. It is not the elders who provide the hero's welcome, but none other than his unnamed and only daughter (11:34).[13] The rashness of his vow meets him full force, its crushing reality juxtaposed with his daughter's exuberant celebration of her father's victory and homecoming. Upon seeing his daughter, the first person to come from his doors, his anguish is apparent, "Alas, my daughter! You have brought me very low; you have become the cause of great trouble to me. For I have opened my mouth to the Lord, and I cannot take back my vow" (11:35). Had Jephthah been separated from his cultural heritage so long that he forgot "the elements of drum, dance, and song [which] constitute a women's performance genre: the musical celebration of military victory"?[14] This tradition within Israel had extended back to the performance of Miriam, the sister of Moses, punctuating Yahweh's victory over the Egyptians at the Red Sea.[15]

Commentators offer different explanations for the justification of Jephthah's vow. Some propose that Jephthah envisioned an animal rather than his daughter as the first "whatever" to exit his abode.[16] This position attempts to align Jephthah with the sacrificial traditions of ancient Israel.[17] Others suggest that the vow captures the extent of foreign influence in Jephthah's life, particularly the practice of human sacrifice.[18] Alice Logan makes the claim that Jephthah's vow is within keeping of an early Israelite tradition where the national leader made a war vow to Yahweh in exchange for national favor.[19] Dennis T. Olson contends that the ambiguous language was intended by the author of Judges.[20] Susan Niditch argues, "The case has been made that Jephthah should have or must have known who would greet him. He is either a rash fool or a conscious practitioner of human sacrifice."[21] As a pastoral psychologist, I wonder if it is possible that Jephthah, having witnessed the human sacrifices to the Ammonites' god Chemosh, believed their rituals better suited his desperate appeal for Yahweh's assistance?[22] Alternatively, does the vow reflect a deeper subconscious longing, the manifestation of the painful existence of Jephthah's rejection and exclusion from his community, such that the need for belonging makes the irrationality of the vow escape him? Barry Webb's conclusions capture the acuity of what this vow means for Jephthah when he states,

Jephthah has everything to lose if the battle goes against him, including his life (see 12:3), but also his position in his clan and tribe, and that clearly means a lot to him. Formerly an outcast, he is now the head and leader of the inhabitants of Gilead. But if he loses the war, the whole cycle of rejection will begin again. If Yahweh rejects Jephthah now, so, too, will Jephthah's people. He will be an outcast once again.[23]

Theoretically, Jephthah's need for belonging harkens back to the absence of a supportive home environment. He lacked the support of parental guidance and mirrors this lack of support when he emphasizes the effect his own words have on him rather than the effect they will have on his daughter. In essence,

Jephthah is oblivious to the impact of the vow on her life. Trent Butler is spot on when he states, "His words betray a patriarchal, self-centered perspective as he accuses the daughter of making him 'bend over in pain' and 'ruining' him (Judges 11:35)."[24] Ultimately, he fails to realize how the accumulation of his poor choices throughout his life has brought him to this moment. Would a different home environment, particularly the presence of a father (or father figure), have influenced the decisions that Jephthah had to make? An exploration into his emotional life could yield insights into what caused Jephthah to utter such a reckless vow. Moreover, understanding the motivation behind his utterance may allow us to be more sympathetic to him and his situation. Have we ever spoken words that were not carefully thought through and wished we could take them back? And, even if it does not make us sympathetic, perhaps gaining an understanding of what motivated Jephthah to make this vow might cause us to be more empathetic to Jephthah's struggle.

Jephthah's Hierarchy of Human Needs

Psychologist Abraham Maslow developed a theory of human motivation known as the hierarchy of human needs.[25] The basic assumption underlying his theory is that human behavior is strongly driven by the urgency of their needs (i.e., human needs driven by survival and personal achievement). Maslow's pyramid is a progressive structure, with the most basic needs at the base of the pyramid ascending upwards to higher needs at the top of the pyramid. The first tier, fundamental to all humans, is the need for food, shelter, clothing, water, air, and sleep, which are essential for the sustenance of life. The second tier addresses the need for safety and security. The third tier includes social needs such as love, affection, friendship, and acceptance by a group. Once these levels of motivation are fulfilled, individuals move on to the fourth tier, self-esteem (self-respect, self-confidence, status, recognition, approval, appreciation). The top tier represents the need for self-actualization (self-development, self-advancement, independence, pursuing one's passions). Maslow's theory when applied to Jephthah's experience in Judges 11 suggests that at least one of these needs has not been met.

Jephthah's basic needs for shelter, clothing, and food appear met while he is exiled in Tob. Surrounding himself with other men who were outcasts, Jephthah satisfies his need for safety and security. With this band of social outcasts pledging their allegiance to him as their leader and thereby serving as an alternative family structure, Jephthah would experience friendship and acceptance. While this group of outcasts rallied around his leadership, they could not bolster his self-esteem, most likely injured by the accumulative effect of the shame of his mother's profession, his father's absence, and his brothers' rejection leading to his refugee status in Tob. There is something about being accepted by one's own family and community that cannot compare with the validation received from non-familial others. Jephthah's rejection by his kinsfolks left him with a strong desire to belong. Although he tries to move to a place of self-actualization, he continues to struggle with acceptance and belonging. Who is Jephthah—the son of a zonah and an unnamed Gileadite—for himself and who is he for or to others?[26] Perhaps Jephthah's motivation and need to belong blinds him to the foolhardiness of his vow. Jephthah's issues with identity and belonging offer insight into the plight of some African American males who felt (and still feel) that the absence of their fathers significantly affected their lives.

Reflections on Fatherlessness within Black Families

Raised in a single parent home, Jephthah's experience parallels that of many African American children. Studies of Black families indicate that sixty-four percent of Black children are raised in single-parent households.[27] Sociologist George Murdock provides a definition of what constitutes a family in American society. He defines the family as a social group that shares a common residence, economic cooperation, and reproduction.[28] For him, the ideal family consists of a married male who is the head of the household, his wife, and their children. He submits that this structure constitutes the traditional family model that sustains a healthy American society. However, the lived experience of most African American children deviates from this norm, which defies the normalization of Western European constructions of family. In his book, *Relational Refugees: Alienation and Reincorporation in African American Churches and Communities*, Edward Wimberly contends that there is stigma attached to those who grow up in female-led single-parent households where the father is absent. He continues, "This stigma is rooted primarily in the high value that the dominant culture places on the nuclear family . . . defining a family exclusively as mom, dad, and two kids leaves many out and contributes to the creation of relational refugees among those who do not meet this standard."[29] The stigma of being a relational refugee has direct implications upon the social and emotional well-being of many African American children who grow up in homes where the father is absent emotionally and physically or both.

Fatherlessness affects African American children socially, emotionally, psychologically, and spiritually, regardless of their gender.[30] Children who grow up in single-parent homes where the father is absent (emotionally or physically) face challenges that impact their development well into adulthood. Fatherlessness and its effects are not specific to gender. Yet, these effects are experienced differently based on gendered needs. While African American females also pay a high price for fatherlessness in their lives, the examination herein is narrowly confined to the way African American males experience this phenomenon. The implications for African American females are beyond the scope of this essay, but I acknowledge the need for further study in this area.

For African American males, the absence of the father figure can have a profound influence upon the individual's ability to meet their basic needs and reach the higher parts of Maslow's hierarchy of needs. Social scientists have demonstrated the challenges that African American children (males) experience when a father is absent from the home. Data suggests that fatherless homes are four times as likely to be poor.[31] Besides the issue of economics, children in fatherless homes are more inclined to engage in drug and alcohol use.[32] According to research conducted at Columbia University, teens in single-parent households headed by women are at 30% higher risk of engaging in smoking, drinking, or use of drugs than teens raised in two-parent households.[33] In addition, studies reveal that children of single-parent homes are predisposed to behavioral problems,[34] twice as likely to die by suicide,[35] and more likely to exhibit aggressive, hypermasculine behaviors.[36] Moreover, these concerns extend to educational achievement. According to sociologist Kathryn Tillman, "Youth that experienced divorce, separation, or non-union birth reported lower grade point averages than those who have always lived with both biological parents."[37] In homes where a father participated in the child(ren)'s education, there was evidence of higher academic achievement.[38] Edward Kruk contends that 71 percent of those who drop out of school come from fatherless homes.[39] His study revealed that these children scored lower on academic achievement tests in reading, math, and critical thinking skills.[40] Comparatively, in studies where the father was present, children were less inclined to engage in delinquency and violence. In these instances, children benefited from the division of parental labor that allowed for parental involvement, supervision, and monitoring, unlike single-parent households that had to negotiate the full breadth of these responsibilities alone.[41] And finally, youth in homes where the father is absent emotionally or physically are more likely to be sexually active during their adolescent years.[42] The above observations are not an attempt to pathologize single-parent households. Instead, we draw attention to the specific issues that occur within single-parent households to enable church leadership to understand that these households may require additional support services such as counseling and/or tutoring.

Recognizing the vital role of fathers in the lives of their children, former president George W. Bush set forth an initiative to address fatherlessness in America. He asserted,

Over the past four decades, fatherlessness has emerged as one of our greatest social problems. We know that children who grow up with absent fathers can suffer lasting damage. They are more likely to end up in poverty or drop out of school, become addicted to drugs, have a child out of wedlock, or end up in prison. Fatherlessness is not the only cause of these things, but our nation must recognize it is an important factor.[43]

African American children who grow up in homes where the father is absent either emotionally or physically often struggle with feelings of abandonment, low self-esteem, and role confusion because they have missed the opportunity to experience the love of an available, nurturing, and caring father. This lack has caused some African American male youth to experience anger, abandonment, and betrayal. In an attempt to drown out the pain and desire for the father, many turn to drugs, alcohol, risky sexual behaviors, unhealthy relationships, gang violence, or other destructive behaviors. For example, Bishop Jonathan Keaton, bishop of the Michigan Area of the United Methodist Church, reflects on his own experience with fatherlessnss and testifies to the Black male's desire for a father. Reflecting on his childhood, he writes,

> In kindergarten, first grade, and Sunday School, my friends and classmates used a word that was beyond my experience: *Father*. "My father did this or my dad did that," they said, or they described a vacation taken with Mom and Dad, a fishing trip with Pops or a Christmas present from Dad. Hearing these oft-repeated narratives set off a spate of questions in my childish mind. Did I have a father? If so, where was he? What was a father?[44]

Bishop Keaton represents just one of many Black males who express their thoughts about growing up without a father. Kevin Greene, an actor and producer who grew up in the projects in

Brooklyn, recounts his experience of growing up without his father:

> Bed-Stuy contributed to the making of the person I came to be. But the absence of the man who was trying to kick down the steel door contributed to who I am far more than my environment could have ever done. That man was my father. I have no memory of him, his personality, or even his face. As far as I'm concerned, we never met . . . Had I been raised by a loving positive father whom I idolized and confided in, I would've been a different person coming up regardless of my environment. My self-worth wouldn't have [sic] been about dealing drugs. My respect for women would not have allowed me to use them. And my many other choices would've been made after a completely different kind of thinking process. Yes, losing my ex's father was tough, but the lesson learned was an indisputable fact: No boy should ever be raised without his father! . . . I see brothers, six to sixty, suffering severely from the transparent unidentifiable wounds I call fatherlessness: and they have absolutely no idea that they're in pain. This is a cancer eating away an entire culture. The only cure is responsibility.[45]

The narrative of so many Black males experiencing a life where there is the absence of the father is troubling at best, and startling when one thinks of the next generation of Black males. Leonard Pitts Jr. developed the term "no-fault fatherhood" to describe the fact that fatherlessness is so prevalent in society, but particularly that it is so acceptable in the Black community. He writes a scathing critique of society's normalization of fatherlessness.

It has become increasingly obvious to me that much of what ails us as African Americans, and us as Americans of whatever heritage, traces from to the simple fact that we have embraced what I will call "no-fault fatherhood." Meaning that fathers are allowed to be only tenuously connected to their families, if at all, allowed to be drop-in visitors on their children if they are there at all, with no social stigma attached to this behavior, no sense of failure or shame. No-fault fatherhood is the new normal.[46]

Thus, the prevalence of fatherlessness in the African American community carries with it dire consequences for the Black male youth who are currently living this reality, and it will have future impact for those yet born.

The Psychological Effects of Mourning in Relation to Fatherlessness

Drawing upon psychologist J. William Worden's work on grief, I would like to suggest the following "prescription" to deal with the grief that fatherlessness can or has caused. Worden outlines a pathway for doing grief work that he calls the Four Tasks of Mourning.[47] Here, I broaden the understanding of grief and loss beyond normative associations with death to include non-death instances of loss (i.e., loss of relationship, job, material, or role). The *first* task of mourning is for fatherless males to come to terms with the reality of the loss.[48] The desire to have one's biological father or father-like figure in one's life and to never have that desire quite fulfilled can be a major deprivation in the life of a young person. This loss can engender pain and emotional discomfort. Kenneth Mitchell and Herbert Anderson accurately acknowledge that so often when it comes to the subject of grief and loss, we tend to only think of it in terms of losing a loved one to death.[49] Their observations suggest that African American males growing up without a father experience loss similar to those who lose someone to death. For the young person, this loss needs to be acknowledged as such. In essence, the youth's denial must give way to acknowledgement and acceptance that the father or father-like figure is not available and will not be available to formulate a nurturing relationship. Once this loss is acknowledged, the youth will experience the floodgate of emotions (sorrow, pain, anger, and betrayal) that come with its acceptance.

The second task of mourning is to experience the pain of grief.[50] This pain is the pain that one would feel in one's body if injured. Then, there is the emotional and psychological pain that the mind seeks to reconcile, often conceptualized as a broken heart. It is the pain and disappointment of having an unfulfilled intense desire for a father or father-like individual in one's life. The desired emotional bond of attachment has been unfulfilled by the reality that one's desire for the father or father-like individual will not come to fruition and will need to be given voice and accepted. The sadness, the pain, the sorrow, and even the anger must be let in and expressed. These sentiments of anger and resentment resonate in Kevin Greene's personal testimony of his absent father, which bears repeating here, "I have no memory of [my father], his personality, or even his face. As far as I'm concerned, we never met. . . Had I been raised by a loving positive father whom I idolized and confided in, I would've been a different person coming up regardless of my environment."[51] According to Worden, if the person resists experiencing the pain through remaining in denial, it will manifest itself in some other form of aberrant behavior (use of drugs, alcohol, or illicit sex) as a means of drowning out one's pain. The youth might seek to avoid the pain of not having a father by creating an imaginary image of the wished-for father, idealizing the absent father or totally negating his desire for the father while all along harboring feelings of resentment and pain.

The third task of mourning is to adjust to an environment in which the desired father or father-like figure is missing.[52] Father-son activities that may have been envisioned as being delegated to fathers need to be adjusted.[53] A recent study noted that in many cultures, fathers tend to fulfill three essential roles: protector, provider, and disciplinarian.[54] While mothers also participate in these roles, it is most often the father who assumes these duties in the traditional patriarchal model of the nuclear family. With the absence of father/father-like figures, adjustments need to be made that fill the gap of the absent other and ensure that male youth receive the guidance and support they need. However, there is another step here that needs to be taken: For the child to come to a sense of peace, he must forgive the father/father-like figure for what is perceived as abandoning him, causing him pain and sorrow, and missing opportunities to bond. Jerrod Brown asserts: "Children who grow up without their fathers may come to resent paternal-figures due to perceived abandonment. These feelings may burgeon from a lack of trust and result in a heightened sense of anger."[55] These feelings, whether conscious or unconscious, will affect the behavior of the child and thus will need to be addressed through the process of forgiveness. Here I draw upon the work of social psychologist Robert Enright that offers a pathway for moving through the forgiveness process.

Robert Enright, in *Forgiveness Is a Choice*, offers specific criteria for the process of forgiving.[56] Applying Enright's criteria to male youth and the issue of fatherlessness results in the following actions. First, the youth must acknowledge that the father's absence is unresolvable (there is not and will never be a relationship between the two). In essence, there were missed opportunities for the father to bond with his son that did not occur because of the father's absence. Second, the youth's anger regarding the father's absence is justified, and he is entitled to claim that anger rather than suppress it. Third, while the anger is justified, the youth must make a conscious decision to give up the right to be angry or resentful towards the father or father figure. At the end of this process, the youth comes to the place where he can let it go.

Enright concludes, "Forgiveness is an act of mercy toward an offender (the desired father or father-like individual), someone who does not necessarily deserve our mercy. It is a gift to our offender for the purpose of changing the relationship between ourselves and those who have hurt us."[57] In the context of fatherlessness, children who are abandoned by their fathers for whatever reason must be informed about the nature of forgiveness in concrete terms appropriate for their age. Their desire to have their fathers in their lives is real and valid. This leads the child directly into the fourth step, which is becoming receptive and embracing a new relationship.

The fourth task is to withdraw emotional energy and reinvest it in another relationship.[58] The powerful desire for a father/father-like figure can consume a youth's emotional energy. The desire for the bond remains, but the possibility of actual occurrence of a bond is dismal or non-existent. In this fourth task, the young man expends his energy of desire. Now, he can open himself to a new relationship, one established through mentorship from a reliable positive male role model who fulfills both his physical and emotional need for a father. As male youth move through this final task, the Church can support them as they heal by providing opportunities for mentoring.

Response of the Black Church: "Each One Reach One: Mentoring"

While Judges 11 does not specifically mention the household, the narrative context leaves open the perception that suggests that Jephthah was raised in a single parent home by his mother, a sex worker. His father, "the Gileadite," appears to have very little involvement (if any) in Jephthah's upbringing and development. The absence of a dominant male figure in Jephthah's life may have contributed to the actions of his half-brothers who disown him, his subsequent involvement with outlaws as a means of supporting himself, and the uttering of a foolish vow to address his need to belong. His father's lack of involvement in his life left room for Jephthah to seek other ways of getting his needs met. This may resonate with the lived experience of many African American males who grow up in homes where the father is absent. Does the church have a role in helping alleviate the negative effects of fatherlessness on young Black males and their integration into the community and society? Here, I offer a prescriptive pastoral care intervention that seeks to ameliorate the problem by identifying an existing resource within many Black Churches, namely, mentorship. African American pastoral theologian Lee Butler Jr. writes that

> Mentoring is a teaching-learning relationship grounded in growth and mutual respect. It is a covenantal relationship rooted in trust. The mentor and mentee form a bond of commitment that declares they will face all of life's challenges together. Without this bond of trust, a mentoring relationship will be short-lived. Mentoring is understood to be a supportive relationship that does not have family ties as its foundation. In some instances, it becomes an additional network of support for the family. In other instances, mentoring aids the young man as he seeks to ensure the prosperous future of his growing family.[59]

Admittedly, mentoring Black youth is not a new or novel concept. In fact, some Black Churches engage in mentorship as a ministry focus.[60] Given that Black Churches minister to youth who come from a variety of family constellations—nuclear families, extended families, single parent families, grandparents raising grandchildren families, mentoring within this context can be highly effective. As previously noted, 64 percent of Black children live in single-parent households. For those families that attend church, it is important that pastors and leaders are aware of the unique challenges that these children face when the father is absent from their lives. Pastors and leaders can develop strategies that address this situation and help to mitigate decisions in which the father's absence and the youth's desire for the father or father-like figure leads to destructive behaviors and choices. Here, the use of mentoring may bring healing and wholeness to youths struggling with this relational gap.

Many Black Churches already have established Men's Fellowship Ministries that conduct monthly activities for the men of the church. This group usually consists of all the men of the church who are single, divorced, married, and widowed. They make an excellent pool of potential mentors. If trained, these men could serve as role models for young Black males where the father is absent. For example, Chris McNair has developed a rites of passage program that aims "to teach Black boys what it means to be African American men, spiritually, culturally, and physically. These three dimensions of self are explored thoroughly to infuse the boys with a strong self-image and positive self-esteem by knowing who they are in Christ."[61] A significant component of McNair's rites of passage program is the role of healthy Black men entering into mentoring relationships with young African American males who come from homes where the role of the father is absent, physically or emotionally. He developed a six-week training program to prepare Black adult men to serve as mentors in the lives of young Black males.[62]

The Brother's/Men's Fellowship Ministry of Black churches can adapt McNair's training sessions to equip mature Black males with relational skills to engage in a long-term committed relationship with young Black males. One aspect of the training seeks to bring healing to these older Black males who themselves may have been injured by the dominant society. Another component is to provide them with guidelines informing them of the parameters of their engagement with Black youth and their mothers. Once these mature, older men go through the training process they can then be paired with these youth. The success of this type of intervention requires ongoing supervision and group meetings between the male volunteers and mentored youth over the span of their relationships. The participation and partnering of mature African American men help fill the emotional gap that fatherlessness inflicts upon young Black males. They are a gift to the Church and the families of the young men they mentor.

Conclusion

Sixty-four percent of African American children grow up in single-parent households that lack a father or father-like figure.[63] Like Jephthah's presumably non-existent relationship with his father, many of these youth have no significant male relationship to guide them in their development into mature manhood. Some may harbor conscious or unconscious anger and resentment due to a powerful desire for a paternal relationship that will most likely never come to fruition. I do not want to imply that matrifocal households are pathological due to this absence. However, Black churches are called to recognize the specific challenges that single-parent households encounter and must seek to offer these families the support they need. One supportive measure is to provide African American children growing up in single-parent households the opportunity to develop life-giving relationships established through mentorship. Mentors can play a significant role in the lives of Black males, especially when supporting female single parents in raising their sons.[64]

The pastoral care initiative provided by the Men's Fellowship Ministry of the Black Churches can be a transformative experience. For the older mature males who might find themselves wanting to contribute to the lives of young Black men, mentoring allows them to give back to the community. For younger males, mentoring provides the moral, physical, and spiritual guidance that only a mature Black male can offer. By filling the emotional gap that fatherlessness creates for young Black males, male mentors can be an asset to Black Churches and Black communities and has the enormous potential of reclaiming many of our young Black youth from spiraling downward into lives of destruction. In other words, restoring the fathers through this mentoring initiative can be a decisive factor in saving our sons.

Discussion Questions

- How do the gaps in the narrative of Jephthah leave space for your "sanctified imagination" when interpreting his story? What conclusions do you draw with respect to the text and fatherlessness?

- What challenges might African American males face growing up without a father in their lives?
- Reflecting on Jephthah's story, are there benefits in having fatherless sons mentored by mature African American males? Why or why not?
- What would it take to begin a mentoring program in your church? What would be some of the first steps in the process?

Additional Resources:

Maria Doerfler, *Jephthah's Daughter, Sarah's Son: The Death of Children in Late Antiquity* (University of California Press, 2019).

"Mentoring," 100 Black Men Mentoring, https://100blackmen.org/four-for-the-future/mentoring/.

"My Brother's Keeper Alliance," Obama Foundation, https://www.obama.org/mbka/about-mbka/.

"Why Every Kid Needs a Mentor," Boys and Girls Club of America, November 11, 2021.

Endnotes

1 According to the 2018 American Community Survey, 64 percent of African American children eighteen and under grow up in single parent homes. See https://datacenter.aecf.org/.

2 Daniel Patrick Moynihan, "The Negro Family: The Case for National Action," US Department of Labor, March 1965, https://www.dol.gov/general/aboutdol/history/webid-moynihan.

3 Mallie J. Paschall et al., "Effects of Parenting, Father Absence, and Affiliation with Delinquent Peers on Delinquent Behavior Among African-American Male Adolescents," *Adolescence* 38 (2003): 15–34.

4 Barry G. Webb, *The Book of the Judges* (JSOT Press, 1987), 57.

5 Phyllis Trible notes that Jephthah's father's identity is tied to the territory of Gilead rather than a proper name. See *Texts of Terror: Literary-Feminist Readings of Biblical Narratives* (Fortress Press, 1984), 94.

6 Kimberly D. Russaw, *Revisiting Rahab: Another Look at the Woman of Jericho* (Welsley's Foundery Books, 2021), 17.

7 Schneider suggests that Jephthah's sense of belonging is compounded by the fact that his mother was a zonah/prostitute. This was a profession not highly regarded amongst Israelite cultural norms and would be a character flaw passed on to Jephthah, diminishing his social status within the group. See Schneider, *Berit Olam: Judges*, 163.

8 Wilda Gafney, *Womanist Midrash: A Reintroduction to the Women of the Torah and the Throne* (Westminster John Knox Press 2017), 3.

9 "Issues in Jewish Ethics: Prostitution," Jewish Virtual Library, accessed February 11, 2013, www.jewishvirtuallibrary.org/prostitution-2.

10 Russaw, "Revisiting Rahab," 18.

11 Psychologists Sigmund Freud, Erik Erikson, Abraham Maslow, and John Bowlby each highlight how the need to belong is a fundamental constituent of human beings. See "Need to Belong," *Psychology*, http://psychology.iresearchnet.com/social-psychology/interpersonal-relationships/need-to-belong/.

12 The terms "whoever" or "whatever," are ambiguous in the original Hebrew. Barry Webb agrees with this assertion but contends that the phrase *liqura ti* "to meet me" would be applicable more to a person than an animal. See Barry Webb, *The Book of Judges* (Eerdmans Publishing, 2012), 247.

13 Karla Bohmbach, "Unnamed Jephthah's Daughter," in *Women in Scripture: A Dictionary of Named and Unnamed Women in the Hebrew Bible, the Apocryphal/Deuterocanonical Books and the New Testament*, ed. Carol Meyers et al. (Houghton Mifflin, 2000).

14 Meyers et al., eds., *Women in Scripture*, 189–90.

15 Ibid. See also Phyllis Trible, *Texts of Terror*, 96–103.

16 See Baruch Halpern, *David's Secret Demons: Messiah, Murderer, Traitor, King* (Eerdmans, 2001); David Janzen, *Witch-Hunts, Purity and Social Boundaries: The Expulsion of the Foreign Women in Ezra 9–10* (Sheffield Academic Press, 2002); and Robert Gordis, *The Book of Judges: The Art of Editing* (Brill Press, 1999).

17 Jephthah's vow if made in reference to animal sacrifice would need to be an animal without blemish and not the firstling for that already belonged to Yahweh (Leviticus 22:17–25). Burnt offering (Hebrew, *'olah*; literally, "ascending offering"; Leviticus 1, 6:8–13) could be a herd or flock animal (bull, sheep, or goat) or a bird (dove or pigeon). The whole animal was burned in the altar fire. It was the most extravagant sacrifice because the entirety was given to God. In burning the sacrifice, it was believed that a transformation took place as the flesh of the animal was converted into smoke. Yahweh received the scent of the burning sacrifice as a sweet-smelling savior (Leviticus 1:13). Is it possible that in making this vow to offer an animal sacrifice Jephthah following in the tradition of Israel was trying to curry a favor from Yahweh that would secure for him the much-needed battle with the Ammonites and thus secure his status among his half-brothers and all the Gileadites?

18 See Susan Niditch, *Judges: A Commentary* (Westminster John Knox Press, 2008); Tikva Frymer-Kensky, *In the Wake of the Goddesses: Women, Culture, and Biblical Translation of Pagan Myth* (Free Press, 1992); and Robert Alter, *Ancient Israel: The Former Prophets: Joshua, Judges, Samuel and Kings, a Translation with Commentary* (W. W. Norton & Company, 2013); Claude Marriottini, "Re-reading Judges 11:31: The Sacrifice of Jephthah's Daughter," https://claudemariottini.com/2007/02/19/rereading-judges-1131-the-sacrifice-of-jephthahs-daughter-2/.Specifically, the vow reflects the practice of human sacrifice similar to that but there is another path of interpretation concerning Jephthah's declaration of the vow. Though there is ambiguity around the subject one cannot escape the fact that Jephthah has lived among foreigners. Is it possible that Jephthah has taken on some of their customs? One wonders whether Jephthah had adopted the religious practice of human sacrifice to the gods as religious practice observed by the worshipers of Baals. The practice of offering human sacrifice was associated with god Molech who was the god worshipped by the Ammonites.

19 Alice Logan, "Rehabilitating Jephthah," *Journal of Biblical Literature* 128, no. 4 (2009): 665–85, https://doi.org/10.2307/25610213.

20 Dennis T. Olson, "The Book of Judges," *The New Interpreter's Bible*, vol. 2, (Abingdon Press, 1998), 831–33.

21 Niditch, *Judges, A Commentary*, 134.

22 See footnote above in reference to Molek, the Ammonite god.

23 Barry Webb, *The Book of Judges* (Eerdmans Publishing, 2012), 246.
24 Trent C. Butler, *Judges* (Zondervan, 2014), 291.
25 "Five Kinds of Human Needs Suggested by Abraham Maslow," Your Article Library, accessed May 3, 2020, http://www.yourarticlelibrary.com/humans/5-kinds-of-human-needs-suggested-by-abraham-maslow-with-diagram/25790.
26 Erik Erikson's theory on identity, Erik Erikson, *Identity and the Life Cycle* (Norton, 1994).
27 See data for children in single-parent families by race in the United States. "Kids Count Data Center," The Annie E. Casey Foundation, accessed February 17, 2022, https://datacenter.aecf.org/.
28 George Murdock, *Social Structure* (Macmillan, 1947).
29 Edward Wimberly, *Relational Refugees: Alienation and Reincorporation in African American Churches and Communities* (Abingdon Press, 2000), 93.
30 Lottie Joiner, "The Impact of Absent Fathers on the Mental Health of Black Boys," USC Annenberg, accessed August 2, 2020, https://centerforhealthjournalism.org/fellowships/projects/impact-absent-fathers-mental-health-black-boys.
31 US Census Bureau, "Table C8. Poverty Status, Food Stamp Receipt, and Public Assistance for Children Under 18 Years by Selected Characteristics: 2011," America's Families and Living Arrangements, https://www.census.gov/data/tables/2011/demo/families/cps-2011.html.
32 John P. Hoffmann, "The Community Context of Family Structure and Adolescent Drug Use," *Journal of Marriage and Family* 64, no. 2 (2002): 314–30.
33 "Research and Statistics," Rochester Area Fatherhood Network, accessed April 2, 2022, http://www.rochesterareafatherhoodnetwork.org/statistics.
34 Sandra Hofferth, "Residential Father Family Type and Child Well-Being: Investment Versus Selection," *Demography* 43, no. 1 (2006): 53–78.
35 Jennifer Rainey, "Suicide Warning Signs: What to Do and Watch For," WebMD, https://www.webmd.com/depression/depression-recognizing-signs-of-suicide.
36 Cynthia Osborne and Sara McLanahan, "Partnership Instability and Child Well-Being," *Journal of Marriage and Family* 69, no. 4 (2007): 1065–83.

37 Kathryn Tillman, “Family Structure Pathways and Academic Disadvantage Among Adolescents in Stepfamilies,” *Sociological Inquiry* 77, no. 3 (2007).

38 Tillman, “Family Structure Pathways.” A study conducted on the involvement of mother and father in the academic achievement of children reported having a male figure—whether biological father, stepfather, or a single parent father—showed father involvement critical to children’s success in school.

39 Edward Kruk, “Father Absence, Father Deficit, Father Hunger: The Vital Importance of Paternal Presence in Children’s Lives,” *Psychology Today*, May 23, 2013, http://www.psychologytoday.com/blog/co-parenting-after-divorce/201205/father-absence-father-deficit-father-hunger.

40 Kruk, “Father Absence.”

41 Stephen Demuth and Susan L. Brown, “Family Structure, Family Process, and Adolescent Delinquency: The Significance of Parental Absence Versus Parental Gender,” *Journal of Research in Crime and Delinquency* 41, no.1 (2004): 58–81.

42 Jane Mendle et al., “Associations Between Father Absence and Age of First Sexual Intercourse,” *Child Development* 80, no. 5 (2009): 1463–80.

43 Office of the Press Secretary, “President Bush Speaks at the Fourth National Summit on Fatherhood,” news release, June 7, 2001, https://georgewbush-whitehouse.archives.gov/news/releases/2001/06/text/20010607-3.html.

44 Jonathan D. Keaton and Ernest S. Lyght, *Our Father: Where Are the Fathers?* (Abingdon Press, 2012), 30.

45 Dawn Marie Daniels and Candace Sandy, eds., *Souls of My Brothers: Black Men Break Their Silence, Tell their Truths, and Heal Our Spirits* (Plume Books, 2003).

46 Leonard Pitts Jr., *Becoming Dad: Black Men and the Journey to Fatherhood* (Agate Books, 2006).

47 While Worden’s work does not specifically address the issue of fatherlessness, his observations can be applied to the present context of fatherless youth and the mourning process. The implementation of these tasks can allow male youth to regain some semblance of healing from the wound of loss that fatherless children experience.

48 Worden, *Grief Counseling and Grief Therapy*, 11–13.

49 Kenneth R. Mitchell and Herbert Anderson, *All Our Losses, All Our Griefs: Resources for Pastoral Care* (Westminster Press, 1983), 18.

50 Ibid., 13–14.

51 Daniels and Sandy, eds., *Souls of My Brothers*.

52 Worden, *Grief Counseling and Grief Therapy*, 14–15.

53 Here I am referring to father-and-son activities which requires the involvement of dads in Cub Scouts (taking fishing trips, learning to tie a tie, camping, playing a game of catch, building pinewood derby car, going to sporting events) and general activities like giving driving lessons, offering dating advice, taking trips to the barbershop, grilling outdoors, playing board games, etc.

54 J. Neil Tift, "What Are the Three Primary Roles of a Father?," https://www.continued.com/early-childhood-education/ask-the-experts/what-three-primary-roles-father-23462.

55 Jerrod Brown, "Father-Absent Homes: Implications for Criminal Justice and Mental Health Professionals," Minnesota Psychological Association, accessed March 31, 2022, https://www.mnpsych.org/index.php%3Foption%3Dcom_dailyplanetblog%26view%3Dentry%26category%3Dindustry%2520news%26id%3D54.

56 Robert Enright, *Forgiveness Is a Choice: A Step-by-Step Process of Resolving Anger and Restoring Hope* (APA LifeTools, 2019).

57 Ibid.

58 Ibid., 15–16.

59 Lee Butler Jr., *Listen My Son: Wisdom to Help African American Fathers* (Abingdon Press, 2010), 34.

60 Andrew Billingsley, *Mighty Like a River: The Black Church and Social Reform* (Oxford University Press, 1999).

61 Chris McNair, *Young Lions: Christian Rites of Passage for African American Young Men* (Abingdon Press, 2001).

62 For the full mentor training program preparing Black men to serve as mentors to young Black males see McNair, *Young Lions*, 42–69.

63 "Black Children, Two-Parent Households, and Black Fatherhood," Black Demographics, https://blackdemographics.com/data-black-children-two-parent-households-and-black-fatherhood/.

64 Nancy Boyd-Franklin, *Black Families in Therapy*, 2nd ed. (Guilford Press, 2003).

5

Nurturing the Disruptive Voice: Naaman's Slave Girl (2 King 5) and the Voices of African American and Afro-Caribbean Immigrant Girls

Janice McLean-Farrell
and Terry Ann Smith

In 2 Kings 5, Naaman's unnamed servant girl offers us a portrait of how the voices of young people can disrupt the status quo. In the text, Naaman's unnamed servant represents the powerless and he the powerful. Many have commented on her situation as a victim or casualty of war.[1] Engaging with research on the resilience of children affected by war, Paba Nidhani De Andrado presents an alternative interpretation of the narrative in which she acknowledges the young servant's traumatic experience yet perceives the girl's words as a resilient expression that validates her cultural identity, principles, and convictions. She writes: "Resilience may be defined as the process of coping and adapting well in the face of adversity, trauma, tragedy, threats, or significant sources of stress . . . resilience appears to be added by agency, whether in the form of external interventions or self-initiated actions/choices."[2] We concur. Reading this text from our own social locations as African American and Jamaican American women, we veer somewhat from interpretations of the biblical story that rightly address issues of gender-based violence, injustice, and psychological terror (i.e., PTSD, Stockholm Syndrome, Rape Trauma Syndrome). In this narrative, we marvel at the young girl's courage and her words. Therefore, rather than just seeing her as a victim of her situation, we also see her as a force for change whose sense of agency significantly alters the trajectory of one man's life. In other words, we elect to read the story in the context of advocacy and empowerment. In doing so, we admit both the sparseness of textual references to the young servant girl and our own intuitions and cultural assumptions that underlie our reading. Nevertheless, we accept the risk of oversimplification and generalizations that attend our reading in order to accentuate the concept of agency and advocacy and the power it possesses in shifting the power dynamics, if only briefly, in this story. Here, the young servant's query to her captors sets Naaman on the road to his healing. We ask what kind of parenting or other support systems might have allowed this young girl to develop and foster a voice that enables her to speak in the same space of her oppression? We surmise that this young girl was possibly raised in an environment that intentionally recognized her voice and cultivated its use.

Comparatively, in Western society (specifically the United States), African American and Black immigrant girls (Afro-Caribbean) are often socialized in spaces where their voices are negated due to discriminatory experiences based on their gender, race, economics, and sexual orientation. In these spaces, many girls are also socialized throughout their childhoods to ignore their pain, stifle their struggles, and bear the oppressions and numerous sexual, racial, and economic microaggressions in silence. In 2 Kings 5, this young Israelite's response to her oppressor's predicament can serve to disrupt stereotypical Western understandings of Black girls' *sassiness* or her *facetiness* (a Jamaican term for a child who talks back) as aggressive behavior and instead offer a new perspective on how Black girls recognize, own, and use their voices. Unfortunately, one consequence of negating African American and Black immigrant girls' voices is their waning self-confidence. As a pastoral care concern, Black churches must understand how fostering parenting in a new way, undoing systems of oppression within the church, and mentoring can ignite the agency of young Black and immigrant girls, thereby equipping and empowering them to overcome the challenges they will most surely encounter as they mature into womanhood.

A Young Girl Speaks Up

Naaman's servant girl receives only a brief mention in 2 Kings 5. Of the twenty-seven verses in chapter five, she makes two appearances. In the first appearance, the narrator records her words as direct speech, while in the second, she is the subject of someone else's comments (2 Kings 5:3, 4). This sparseness is a clear indication that the story is not about her. The account is essentially about men, men's politics, and God intervening in men's affairs. Christine Mitchell concludes that the young girl's slave identity is "unremarkable to the narrative, an everyday reality of the violence that helps realize the imperial dream."[3] In other words, the young girl is a bit player, an extra written in and written out, or a pawn used strategically to move the main protagonist, Naaman, forward. Yet, her identity as an enslaved person is precisely what makes her an exceptional figure in this story. Moreover, given the biblical tendency to objectify girls and women, the young servant's significance to the narrative plot becomes all the more striking.

The story's initial backdrop takes place behind enemy lines and begins with a non-Israelite, a foreigner who is himself subject to a higher authority. Her captor, Naaman, is the commander of the Syrian army (5:1). He is described as "a great man" and "mighty warrior," a man highly esteemed by an unnamed Syrian king.[4] Yet, beneath this veneer of respectability, one suspects a life marred by war and violence. Moreover, despite his powerful status, the commander suffers from a skin disease.[5] Naaman's marred physical appearance disrupts the narration of his impeccable character and social standing. The narrator juxtaposes Naaman's status with the status of the young Israelite girl, a prisoner of war. "Now the Arameans on one of their raids had taken a young girl captive from the land of Israel, and she served Naaman's wife" (5:2). Sidney Berman draws a contrast between Naaman and this servant in which "great comes against small, Aramean against Israelite, conqueror against captive, male against female, adult against child, ruler against servant and famous against unnamed."[6] Julie Parker provides a similar contrast,

> Naaman and this enslaved person are paradoxically bound through their differences. Both present themselves before someone who they serve, yet they serve on very different levels . . . Naaman has family (v.2), money (v. 5b), horses and chariots (v. 9), and servants (v.13) to accommodate his wishes. The slave girl lacks the security of kin and possessions as she tends to others.[7]

The servant's situation mirrors other biblical references that sanction the taking of women and young girls as spoils of war. For example, in Judges, Sisera's mother, unaware of her son's death, explains his delayed homecoming, "Are they not finding and dividing the spoil? — A girl or two for every man (Judges 5:30).[8] We also find the seizing of young girls as war brides in Judges 21:19–22:

> So they said, "Look, the yearly festival of the Lord is taking place at Shiloh, which is north of Bethel, on the east of the highway that goes up from Bethel to Shechem and south of Lebonah." And they instructed the Benjaminites, saying, "Go and lie in wait in the vineyards and watch; when the young women of Shiloh come out to dance in the dances,

> then come out of the vineyards and each of you carry off a wife for himself from the young women of Shiloh and go to the land of Benjamin. Then if their fathers or their brothers come to complain to us, we will say to them, 'Be generous and allow us to have them, because we did not capture in battle a wife for each man. But neither did you incur guilt by giving your daughters to them.'"

Thus, the biblical material attests that young girls (Israelites and non-Israelites alike) found themselves in tenuous and dangerous situations during times of warfare. As such, it is conceivable that these young girls would have little input or control over their lives, their bodies, or their voices.

In 5:3, we encounter the partial exchange between the enslaved young Israelite and her mistress. "She said to her mistress, 'If only my lord were with the prophet who is in Samaria! He would cure him of his leprosy.'" We do not know how long this young girl has been a servant to Naaman's wife. Her age is uncertain given that biblical narratives lack specificity as it pertains to an age group that corresponds to our modern notions of female development where one transitions from pre-adolescence to adolescence to adulthood. The Hebrew uses the phrase הָנַּטְק הָרֲעַנ (*naarah qetannah* or small girl) to describe the young Israelite. The term הָרֲעַנ *naarah* (girl or damsel) appears variably as a reference to a young woman of marriageable age (see 1 Samuel 9:11, Genesis 24:14, 16; 34:3, 12), female attendants (see Genesis 24:61; Esther 2:9), or a young widow (see Ruth 2:6). However, the addition of the adjective הָנַּטְק *qetannah* (small) suggests that perhaps the term should not be interpreted as a reference to an adult female. Given the above, the most likely translation of the phrase is a "young or small girl." Carolyn Leeb observes that the term הָרֲעַנ *naarah* frequently refers to young servant girls under the supervision of an adult female.[9] Leeb's rendering is appropriate here as it captures a child who may be too young to be exploited as an object of sexual desire, but old enough to serve as a lady's maid.

For some (not all), home is a place of love and security. Young girls (and boys) learn at an early age in the home, or outside of it, whether the world is friend or foe and whom to trust. In essence, young people learn which behaviors are acceptable and unacceptable. According to Erik Erikson, mothers, typically the primary caregivers, are instrumental in creating the bonds of trust forged during the earliest stages of an infant's development. Mothers' consistent attention to the physical (feeding), emotional (cuddling), and spiritual (affirming) needs of their children establishes a trustful sense that all is well. For Erikson, this early attention lays the foundation upon which other positive developmental areas can build or become negative outcomes that challenge the psychosocial development of the individual well into adulthood.[10]

Before becoming the servant of Naaman's wife, this young girl most likely lived with her family and extended family. She would stay within the confines of this household structure until she married and became part of her husband's family. Moving within the gendered spaces where women's activities (baking, weaving, etc.) took place, she would have listened, learned, and interacted with other young girls and women.[11] Perhaps she would have heard how Rebekah surreptitiously secured the birthright for her favorite son Isaac (Genesis 27:5–10) or how Rachel used the excuse of her menstrual cycle to retain the household gods as she relocated to a new home with her husband, Jacob (Genesis 31:33–35). During these interactions with other women, she possibly heard the oral tales about the widow Tamar, who spoke out to restore her honor and ensure that she received justice (Genesis 38:24–26). She would have heard the story of how a young girl watched over the baby Moses and suggested to Pharoah's daughter that his own mother nurse him (Exodus 2:4–8). For the young Israelite, these gendered spaces within her mother's house and nested within the larger household of her father may have been where she learned that her voice was important, that her actions could impact the lives of others, and that her truth was not dependent on the claims others made about her. This young girl would have learned about the faith and courage of these women as well as the examples set by the women in her context. Perhaps she learned that when women (and girls) speak up, they affect and influence those around them.[12]

Unlike Hagar, another young girl given to serve someone else's needs (and perhaps herself a prisoner of war) whose voice is muted, Naaman's unnamed servant speaks directly to her captors.[13] She said to her mistress, "If only my lord were with the prophet who is in Samaria! He would cure him of his leprosy" (5:3). Some commentators attribute the young girl's solution to Naaman's predicament to the amicable relationship between her and her mistress.[14] Or does the young girl's care and concern for her captor depict the moral values embedded in her faith? These conclusions represent various interpretations and explanations for the young girl's motives. However, they tend to privilege Naaman's healing and his impending encounter with Elisha and pay little attention to the girl's status as a prisoner of war living among foreigners.

Altogether, these are certainly plausible readings of the story. Yet, they make the young girl complicit in her own oppression. That is, these conclusions presuppose that she has adjusted to her servitude such that she now puts her oppressors' needs above her own. Furthermore, they do not account for the traumatic experience of war nor for how her words empower and (possibly) protect her. Consider the story of Daniel and his compatriots, young boys from elite families taken into exile by the Babylonians to serve in the king's palace. Speaking directly to their captors, they resist assimilation by carefully choosing words that result in a substitute meal plan that allows them to eat their preferred food (Daniel 1:11–16). Daniel and his countrymen go on to succeed in the king's court, but they always live under the threat that their freedom could be undone at any moment. Speculatively, Naaman's Israelite servant, like Daniel and his compatriots, may have come from an elite family and may have then been placed in service to an elite family when her home was raided. Perhaps this young girl learned long before these young boys that not only are words powerful, but also that words spoken at the right time and in the right context can be liberating.

Notably, the exchange in 2 Kings 5:3 features the girl's words and not those of her mistress as she becomes the first person to speak in the story. The constraints of her position do not negate the priority the narrator gives to her voice. Instead, her perspective exudes a kind of wisdom and integrity that is not reticent or reserved. This young person expresses an awareness of Naaman's predicament and puts forth a solution. She offers Naaman what he has taken from her, her freedom. She was not sold to this elite household; she was forcibly removed from her home. She is an orphan dependent on the benevolence of her captors for sustenance and survival. Furthermore, their benevolence does not change her status, a servant in a foreign household in a foreign land. When and under what circumstances might she gain her freedom? Freedom comes in many forms (i.e., freedom from something, freedom to do something, and freedom to be somebody). The imaginative reality of her freedom is perhaps out of reach; however, the same is not true for her captor.

For Naaman, freedom is the release from his diseased condition. The servant's simple "if only" are words that project a contemplative musing, an assertiveness that is non-threatening but that attests to her resilience despite her circumstances. Her response, according to De Andrado, "does not count as evidence of her subjection to her captors' coercive control or her adaptation to an abusive situation . . . On the contrary, the girl strives to expose the hollowness of the priorities of her master's world, and to establish the primacy of her own values."[15] Going further, she states that, "Despite the forced uprooting from her social ecology, the girl retains those tenets inculcated into her in her native land."[16] This early formation is crucial as she retains her identity in the midst of powerful foreigners. And, perhaps for the briefest moment, the pendulum of power shifts as this young Israelite's discernment and knowledge of the prophet empowers her while simultaneously disempowering her owners, who do not have access to the hidden transcripts of the enslaved or the channels that connect them.[17] She does not name the prophet, only his location and capabilities. She may have learned of him through the witnesses and testimony of other Israelite adults who had encountered him. Comparatively, the Syrian commander and his wife have never heard of him. Jean Kyong Kim submits, "the little girl's remark moves from low to high until her words finally come before the highest, the king of Aram" (5:4, 5).[18] Therefore, despite her minimal presence, her words serve as the cornerstone from which all other characters in the narrative draw their guidance.

To what or whom might we attribute her candid interjection? In his book *The Moral Intelligence of Children*, Robert Coles posits that children learn through witnessing adults.

> We grow morally as a consequence of learning how to be with others, how to behave in this world, a learning prompted by taking to heart what we have seen and heard. The child is a witness; the child is an ever-attentive witness of grown-up morality—or lack thereof; the child looks and looks for cues as to how one ought to behave, and finds them galore as we parents and teachers go about our lives, making choices, addressing people, showing in action our rock-bottom assumptions, desires, and values, and thereby telling those young observers much more than we realize.[19]

For the most part, biblical narratives contain little information on the treatment of children in ancient Israel. At times, children appear as economic commodities (Exodus 21:7, 2 Kings 4:1, Nehemiah 5:5). In other instances, they seem highly regarded and valued (Deuteronomy 18:10; Psalms 127:3–5, 128:3–6). Still, in other portraits, they are the objects of violence and abuse (Genesis 22:9; Exodus 1:16; Isaiah 13:16; Psalm 137:9). Yet, despite the paucity of evidence, we can glean some knowledge about the role of mothers in the lives of their children. For example, mothers are the predominant educators who socialize young girls and boys into Israelite culture and traditions (Exodus 2:7–11;

Nehemiah 13:23, 24; 1 Samuel 1:22–28; Proverbs 1:8). Mothers (and fathers) serve as marriage negotiators for their daughters (Genesis 21:21; 24:28, 55). Some young women negotiated their own marriages (Numbers 36:6). Despite Ezekiel's negative portrayal of women in 16:44, he hints at a kind of "girl power," or knowledge young girls glean from their mothers. Naomi's instructions to Ruth before appearing on the threshing floor suggest that perhaps Naomi received similar guidance in her youth (Ruth 3:3, 4). These examples advance the proposition that a young girl's early formation (knowledge of the world and others, behavior, attitude, etc.) begins with instruction by their mothers or other maternal figures. Although the biblical text is silent on the formative years of the young Israelite prior to her capture by Naaman, archaeological evidence of households in ancient Israel provides glimpses into the use and function of gendered spaces from which theoretical conclusions regarding the socialization of children may be drawn.[20]

Naaman's servant quickly fades from our and the narrator's purview. Still, it is possible to speculate that the young Israelite's response to her mistress's situation reflects an agency and assertiveness cultivated long before her present state as someone's property. There is a lesson in her story for those involved in youth ministry in Black churches, particularly when working with young African American and Afro-Caribbean immigrant girls. Nurturing the voices of young African American and Afro-Caribbean immigrant girls can promote positive and healthy self-images that allow them to speak not only into their situations but also into the situations of those like them.

Young Girls Owning Their Voices

The young Israelite servant is a foreigner in the land of Syria who has a cultural distinctiveness that sets her apart from her captors. We imagine that her socialization most likely occurred among the mothers and other women who performed the essential tasks necessary to maintain their households.[21] Comparatively, the process young African American and Afro-Caribbean immigrant girls undergo in discovering, owning, and using their voices can be a daunting one. Perhaps, somewhat like ancient Israel, it requires the intentionality of adults—particularly mothers and fathers—to create and maintain a sacred space for this process. Stated differently, the creation and maintenance of a sacred space does not occur in a vacuum but within a particular context, with accompanying socialization practices and behaviors that in turn shape both the expectations and trajectories of African American and Afro-Caribbean immigrant girls.

What then is this context? Regardless of their geographical (urban, suburban, rural) and socioeconomic conditions (lower, middle, upper, below the poverty line, etc.) and familial (nuclear, extended, single parent, guardian of the state, etc.) or cultural backgrounds (African American, immigrant, mixed race, etc.), these young girls are coming of age in a racialized America. According to Eduardo Bonilla-Silva and Victor Ray, "talking about racism has become quite tricky in contemporary America . . . [It has often] been reduced to prejudice and its overt expressions"[22] as exhibited by a few people like those who participate in the modern US militia movement[23] and evidenced by the January 6, 2021 attack on the Capitol. They argue that this framing is problematic because it discounts that "racism forms a social system in which we all participate. . . . [Such] systems are anchored around real practices, institutions, and subjectivities that produce positions of relative privilege for some and of subordination for others. [These are the same] racial practices, events, behaviors and cognitions in the public sphere [that] have become normative, subtle, institutionalized, and apparently non-racial."[24]

However, the experiences of African American and Afro-Caribbean immigrant girls within American society are not solely racial but also gendered, and thus exhibit interlocking patterns. Christopher Clark posits that these patterns appear in the "[the acquisition of] the knowledge, attitudes, values, and patterns of behavior from which [the young girls] construct their gender identities [and the acceptable forms of] behavior for [their] cultural environment."[25] In essence, patterns of disparities and the negation of young African American and Afro-Caribbean immigrant girls' voices manifest as part of their socialization.[26] As these girls belong to two culturally diverse groups, we focus on the overarching structures that shape the socialization of each group. These spaces of socialization include the *home* (parents, guardians, and other family members as the primary socialization agents) and the *public sphere* (religious spaces). For young Afro-Caribbean girls, it is also necessary to discuss socialization processes in the Caribbean, as Afro-Caribbean parents draw on many of the foundational elements from this context in raising their daughters in the United States.

Socialization of Afro-Caribbean Immigrant Girls

Hyacinth Evans and Rose Davies observe that within the Caribbean, children are highly valued and that "parents, in general, state that they want what is best for their children."[27] This outlook, in turn, shapes parents' child-rearing and socialization practices. Central to these processes are two principles that many parents adhere to: "spare the rod and spoil the child" and "children should be seen and not heard."[28] According to Evans and Davies, "across socioeconomic groups, parents value a punitive, restrictive approach to discipline and childrearing. Obedience and docility are valued especially for girls."[29] Such attention to the obedience of one's daughter is complimented by her socialization along traditional gendered lines. Barry Chevannes observes that within the home, "young girls are expected to receive their training on the instruction and by the example of their mothers [or female figure] around the house."[30] Janice McLean-Farrell extends this thought by noting that in both urban and rural contexts, "young girls are expected to learn how to care for siblings and perform those chores normally associated with the house . . . By participating in these activities, [young girls] learn that they are to care for their homes[s] and children."[31]

As a result, for most girls, femininity is associated with the idea of nurturing, freedom to express emotions, and caring for others.[32] At the same time, some girls, especially those from the middle and upper classes, are socialized to achieve an education and become gainfully employed. Despite the progress in wage equality, for many Caribbean females, patriarchal structures rooted in the traditional socialization processes mentioned above remain firmly in place. These processes include, among others, protecting young girls, especially from early involvement in sexual relationships, conversations regarding their physical development, and how to navigate their emotional and social lives when engaging the dominant society.[33]

Nevertheless, this traditional framing of femininity begins to change as Afro-Caribbean immigrants adapt to life in the United States, where greater emphasis is placed on gender equality. Accompanying this shift is the re-articulation of a masculinity that is not necessarily linked to the man as the primary provider for one's family, and the construction of a femininity that fosters and encourages leadership in the workplace. As a result of this shift, room is made for greater gender parity and collaboration which benefits the entire family. In essence, both parents assume responsibility for child-rearing activities. Even household tasks become non-gendered, avoiding designations that limit girls to cooking and cleaning, and boys to removing the family's trash.

As Afro-Caribbean children come of age in the United States, some parents now realize that given the cultural differences between the Caribbean and the United States, directly importing child-rearing practices from the Caribbean may not work, especially when it comes to practices like corporal punishment and the injunction for children to be seen and not heard. As a result, McLean-Farrell submits that "parents and children are having to work together to discern the way forward. In uncharted territory, many parents are becoming more open to the input of their children regarding their socialization and the wider cultural principles surrounding equality."[34] Immigrant children, especially those within working class African American neighborhoods, often adhere to immigrant-specific identities as a way of separating themselves from the dominant media and public stereotypes often associated with African American youth, particularly those from low-income neighborhoods.[35] As a result, many of the cultural practices appropriated while Afro-Caribbeans assimilate also aligns with the values of white middle-class Americans, a reflection and projection of their assimilation.[36]

Socialization of African American Girls

Like their Afro-Caribbean counterparts, African American girls are also loved and valued within their families. However, racism remains an ever-present reality and thus affects the lives of all African American children. Given the threats and assaults against Black bodies and insidious attempts to undermine Black identity in American society, Black parents strive diligently to counter the negative stereotypical narratives of the dominant majority and instill their children with a sense of Black pride.[37] For Desire Shenay Taylor, this includes "buffer[ing], filter[ing], and interpret[ing] negative messages regarding Black humanity."[38] According to Nancy Boyd-Franklyn, some parents seek to compensate for this reality by socializing their daughters and sons in different ways.[39] While such differentiation may be valid, she notes that it "contributes to the often sexist, victimizing, and contradictory messages that Black men and women receive."[40] For African American girls, education is also a key part of their socialization, as it is seen as one of the primary ways for them to advance within American society. For many African American families, another key aspect of young girls' socialization is to raise them "to be fiercely loyal, interdependent with the family, independent, assertive and strong."[41] Mothers or other maternal figures play a significant role in this process as they prepare African American young girls for motherhood. In essence, these mothers or maternal figures prepare young girls to care for their future families, and where coping becomes one mechanism among many that allows them to succeed and survive in a society that at times can be hostile to their presence.

African American young girls' survival within American society is predicated on their knowledge and socialization as a racial minority. In conceptualizing the dynamics that accompany the process of racial socialization, scholars often invoke the triple quandary model developed by A. Wade Boykins, who argues, "The triple quandary presents Afro-Americans with three realms that must be socially negotiated: mainstream American, Black cultural, and oppressed minority." [42] The concern that the values of the white majority do not align with the experiences of African Americans as a minoritized group shows up in how African Americans raise and protect their children, which involves preparing African American children to be successful in oppressive environments.[43] Their success is predicated on Black youth receiving cultural reinforcement through messages that address racial pride while destigmatizing messages that undermine Black heritage, history, and tradition. Proactive messages foster pride and appreciation of African American heritage while protective messages cultivate awareness of racism and biases in the wider society.[44] The combination of this messaging enables African American youth (girls and boys) to navigate and value what it means to be African American in a racialized society.

Respectability Politics, Black Femininity and Black/Afro-Caribbean Churches

Within the African American and Afro-Caribbean community, racialized tropes are sometimes expressed in the form of respectability politics. Respectability politics suggests that emulation of the dominant culture is the path that ensures minoritized groups receive respect and equitable treatment. This view permeates in the wider society and the church, particularly some Black and Afro-Caribbean churches, where respectability politics attends binary framings that promote concepts like the ideal or loose (Afro-Caribbean churches) or lady or ho (Black churches). These binary framings have been unhelpful and demeaning for young girls as they seek to emulate one and avoid the other.

In the Caribbean context, the ideal/loose binary represents the "dual cultural heritage of the Caribbean with Euro and Afro-Caribbean components."[45] With this dualism, upper- and middle-class women adhere primarily to the Eurocentric Victorian ideals equated with status and position within the church and society, thus conforming to the status quo. In contrast, the stigmatization of working-class women, primarily of African descent, occurs because they align with Afro-Caribbean norms. The loss of status and reputation that accompanies this stigmatization leads to labeling these women as loose. McLean-Farrell argues that "this loss of status/reputation in the Caribbean Church (diaspora included) is regained by leaving one's 'loose' lifestyle to become a 'bride of Christ.'"[46] In this process, transformation as the reformed woman takes on the "respectable" qualities exemplified by her middle- or upper-class contemporaries. The implications have direct bearing on their daughters as they witness the marginalizing and potential silencing of their cultural identity in favor of Christian Eurocentric values.

In the Black church context, the coupling of the lady or ho binary assumes and seeks a similar conformity. Tamura Lomax in *Jezebel Unhinged* offers the following analysis of the lady/ho binary and the way it aligns with respectability politics:

> While many black American Christians resist language of mammy, they simultaneously uphold the "virtuous woman" in Proverbs 31:10–31 as an exemplar of womanhood. The parallel is in no way exact. Yet the feminization of virtue in black Christian contexts produced some cross-pollination between the Victorian ideal, respectability politics, and the historical mammy figure that cannot be ignored. Black women of virtue, often interchanged with the black lady trope, are everything jezebel sluts are supposedly not. They are expected to hold a higher moral standard and maintain beauty ideals while nurturing and carrying entire black communities on their backs from sunup to sundown.[47]

For Black churches in the US and the Caribbean, the construction of a counternarrative of Black femininity from the depraved, inherently promiscuous, uncivilized African woman that was trafficked during slavery and beyond has "produced a new picture and alternative power structure [that] did little to lessen the yoke of previous racist sexist politics, epistemes and ideologies."[48] Instead, it has institutionalized the distinction "between who and what was virtuous and not, enabling a culture of gender hierarchy, sexual secrecy, closeting, and policing."[49] This in turn further cemented the "necessity" of the binary tropes it had hoped to displace. As Lomax states, "if cis-gender heterosexual black lady was essential to participating in or performing the black "nuclear" project, the crest of black morality, order, progress, and uplift, then vital to making that narrative stick in neocolonial America [and the Caribbean contexts], at least among black people, was upholding the jezebel/ho/promiscuous trope."[50]

While parents and Black churches can provide young African American and Afro-Caribbean girls with strategies and sacred spaces that help them discover, nurture, and use their voices, this is not always the case as we have noted above. In fact, oftentimes the socializations provided can reinforce systems of oppression and negate the voices of these girls.

Parenting a Black Girl is Justice Work

How can African American/Afro-Caribbean parents and Black/Afro-Caribbean churches disrupt the power structures and gender hierarchy that oppress our daughters? First, we must acknowledge that parenting and spiritual care is occurring in an increasingly divisive society. Today parents must have conversations about police encounters not only with their sons but also with their daughters. These conversations loom large in the context of the murders of Breonna Taylor and Sandra Bland, together with many other unknown daughters whose lives have been cut short through these interactions. We must also be conscious of the over-sexualization of our daughters in the media, our homes, and our churches, while staying ever mindful of their criminalization in our schools. Second, as parents and spiritual care providers, we are complicit in our daughters' oppression. That is, as parents of Black children, we have internalized and subconsciously passed on to our progeny Western, Eurocentric systems of oppression.[51] One example of this survives in the way colorism shapes standards of beauty within African American and Afro-Caribbean families and communities.

For parents and other caregivers, overcoming systems of oppression requires learning to parent our daughters in a new way—as an act of justice! To parent our children in the manner we—especially African American/Afro-Caribbean women—were socialized is to perpetuate the systems of oppression and make our children ill-prepared for the world they will inhabit. For African American/Afro-Caribbean women, it requires the reexamination of our awareness of a particular racial consciousness—the moment we realized that our wombs carry Black bodies that some in America deem destined to die in violent and subtle ways. For McLean-Farrell, this particular racial consciousness came on a warm summer evening in Harlem when she witnessed a young African American male being chased and apprehended by five white NYPD officers. As the onlookers recorded the event, they called for the young man's mother, and I realized that I was her—a Black mother! A critical part of this realization is that in the presence of the white gaze, all our children are the same, regardless of their parents' class, geographical location, education, immigrant status, religious affiliation, etc. As such, none of it, not the respectability politics we engage in, nor the gender hierarchy systems we construct, will be adequate to shield our children from what Ta-Nehisi Coates calls, "the visceral experience [that is racism in America] that dislodges brains, blocks airways, rips muscle, extracts organs, cracks bones, breaks teeth. . . . [It is always remembering] that the sociology, the history, the economics, the graphs, the charts, the regressions all land, with great violence, upon the body," the Black body.[52]

Disruption happens as various cultural hegemonies, systems, structures, and injunctions—"a child should be seen and not heard," and others—are laid aside to make room for our daughters' voices. With this disruption, parenting becomes a more collaborative process, where daughters are encouraged to talk back, to be *facety* and *renk* (Jamaican colloquialisms), and to *sass* (African American context). In this collaborative process, daughters learn to advocate for their needs and express their views. This dialectic process can oftentimes border on disrespect and draw the disdain and criticism of older family members, even members of the wider community who regard such collaborative behavior as improper and unacceptable for a child. When this occurs, parents must become conversation brokers, preserving the sacredness of this collaborative space which encourages the discovery and use of the daughter's voice. Parents must recognize that their homes are one of the few places where their children learn to be their full, authentic selves. The significance of this sacred process demands the death of socialization practices and beliefs that continue to relegate the personhood and voices of girls and women of African descent to the margins, particularly within African American and Afro-Caribbean communities.

This epistemological shift also requires what Emilie Townes calls a countermemory, the "open[ing] up [of] subversive spaces within the dominant discourse that expand our sense of who we are and, possibly, create a more whole and just society in defiance of structural evil."[53] Countermemory processes provide the "reconstitution of history such that we begin to see, hear, and appreciate the diversities in our midst as flesh and blood rather than as cloying distractions within the fantastic hegemonic imagination."[54] This fantastic hegemonic imagination, which is in all of us, according to Townes, "uses a politicized sense of history and memory to create and shape *its* worldview. It sets in motion whirlwinds of images [and stereotypes] used in the cultural production of evil."[55] This imagination allows us to read the subtext latent in the history, laws, politics, images, and worldview of the dominant systems and structures to discern the voices, agency, and resistance of the oppressed. As a result, parents and other caregivers can begin to recover and become re-rooted in the cultural wisdom of our African ancestors, continue the work of justice to alter the effects of oppression, and create a more whole, just world.

Given the inherent dangers that Black children encounter in general, and that our daughters in particular experience in American society, the need to recover and re-root in the cultural wisdom of our ancestors will require passing on the subtle art of "playing the fool to catch the wise." This skill, often exhibited by mythical figures like Anansi and Br'er Rabbit, provides our daughters with the ability to quickly assess a situation, anticipate potential outcomes, and employ their wits, experience, and resources to navigate adversity. An essential aspect of this teaching lies in sharing the stories of how both living and departed "kin" have employed this strategy for survival. By recounting, reflecting on, and celebrating these "kin" stories, parents empower their daughters to build a countermemory. This countermemory helps them maintain their agency and voice while navigating a society that is often hostile to their existence and intent on their marginalization.

Practical Implications for African American and Afro-Caribbean Churches

The task for African American and Afro-Caribbean churches is to foster, encourage, and augment the work of families as they parent for justice on two levels—historical and contemporary. For Black churches, this requires re-engaging their history as the religious institutions of slaves and their role resisting and subverting the oppressive systems and structures (slavery, colonization, Black laws, etc.) that demanded the enslavement, dehumanization, and denigration of Black bodies.[56] In these churches, the seemingly individual processes of raising daughters in a new way—as an act of justice—meet the communal in profound ways. This way of thinking reasserts the long-acknowledged role of the communal in the work of justice, as evidenced in the South African term *ubuntu*, "I am because we are." For Afro-Caribbean churches, it is to re-engage the long history of Blacks (free and enslaved) in undermining the structures of the plantation and society.[57]

Contemporary engagement embraces both prophetic and pastoral dimensions. The prophetic begins by calling out the ways Black churches are complicit with the dominant structures of oppression including the numerous ways Black churches have offered and continue to offer the bodies of their female members on the altars of hierarchy, patriarchy, sexism, respectability, assimilation, class advancement, and theological acceptance. For Afro-Caribbean churches, the challenge is to recognize that some of these Black bodies now worship in the masters' church. Given this reality, the very theological foundation of these churches needs excavation and redemption to facilitate the emancipation of Black bodies in these sacred spaces. Again, Townes is instructive, asserting that "the search for justice must have both manifest and latent functions. The manifest function, our conscious motivation, will vary according to contexts and conditions. . . . The structures and individuals behind the issues we face in ministry reveal the latent function of our work."[58] The work of justice on behalf of individuals in various contexts and conditions is colossal and will not happen quickly or even within some of our lifetimes. It is here that the verses of Hebrews 11:39–40 and 12:1 are instructive; our ancestors in the faith—the witnesses—wait for us to do our part because it is only together that we are made perfect. Therefore, each act of justice, regardless of how small it may seem, is significant in moving us toward transformation.

The pastoral dimensions center on caring and parenting in the Church and in Black and Afro-Caribbean communities. These dimensions acknowledge the trauma Blacks within the transatlantic region have experienced and continue to experience—including what has been inflicted within the sacred walls of the Church. Here, too, context matters and therefore social analysis and a comprehensive consideration of all relevant information is key—including the "humanness of being human."[59] Townes posits:

> We must strive to understand that the personal side of transformation in which people are being changed and renewed requires an entirely different set of critical and analytical skills to affect faithful witness. As agents for agitation seeking to bring in the new heaven and new earth, we can help others find their witness, their voice. Still, we must hold as precious the humanity of all people and the blessedness of creation. We must reach out to others with tenderness, concern, grace, and never forget that the pastoral voice must also be blended with the prophetic voice.[60]

In meeting these pastoral needs, it is important not to trivialize the trauma people have experienced. At the same time, churches need to attend to the ways in which growth can be fostered from trauma. It is here that research from the positive psychology area of post-traumatic growth could be instrumental.[61] When utilizing this data for the Black community and for racial trauma in particular, a process of critical translation is needed since this has been severely understudied in the field.[62] For Black churches to reap the benefits of psychology, the stigma normally associated with counseling, therapy, and psychological interventions needs to be addressed. For young African American and Afro-Caribbean girls, personal transformation requires a communal dimension. Mentoring and rites-of-passage programs like Daughters of Imani, as well as the commitment to engage in the hard conversations about the tensions and divisions that exist among girls and women, are essential.[63]

Conclusion

Returning to Naaman's servant, we find a young girl that has persevered through a traumatic experience in which her voice alone rings out as a possible testimony to the women who raised her. Despite her young age, we detect an agency that is empowering and empowers. Today, there are examples of young people, who, like this young girl of scripture, own their voices. For example, Marley Diaz, a thirteen-year-old, places Black girls at the center of her activist work and writings.[64] Five-year-old Sophie Cruz advocates on behalf of immigrants.[65] We admire their passion and commend the parenting that provided the soil from which their passions sprang forth. Yes, African American and Afro-Caribbean girls are coming of age in a societal "house" that is at times oppressive and dehumanizing. Yet, their homes and churches must become the sacred spaces that enable them to discover, own, and use their voices to disrupt stereotypical images and discourses that undermine their self-esteem; these sacred spaces make their voices and well-being a priority, resulting not only in their own freedom, and the freedom of other young girls, but freedom for their oppressors as well.

Discussion Questions

- What does Naaman's servant girl risk in addressing his situation?
- What conclusions do you draw from Naaman and his wife (adults) taking counsel from this young girl (a child)?
- Discuss the various interpretations that can arise from a contextual reading of this passage? Which one appeals to you and why?
- How would your church go about creating sacred spaces where young girls are encouraged to be their authentic selves?

Additional Resources

Richelle B. White, *Daughters of Imani: Christian Rites of Passage for African American Young Women* (Abingdon Press, 2005).
Anne E. Wimberly and Sarah Frances Farmer, *Raising Hope: Four Paths to Courageous Living for Black Youth* (Baker Books, 2017).

Endnotes

1 Choon-Leong Seow, "1 and 2 Kings," in *The New Interpreter's Bible*, vol. 3 (Abingdon Press, 1998); Gerald West, "Reading Abused Female Bodies in the Bible: Interpretative Strategies for Recognising and Recovering the Stories of Women Inscribed by Violence but Circumscribed by Patriarchal Text (2 Kings 5)," *Old Testament Essays* 15, no. 1 (2002): 240–58.

2 Paba Nidhani De Andrado, "The Resilience of the Captive Girl Child in 2 Kings 5," *Journal for the Study of the Old Testament* 45, no. 4 (2021): 464.

3 Christine Mitchell, "1 and 2 Kings," in *Women's Bible Commentary* (Westminster John Knox Press, 2012), 175.

4 Translations are based on the New Revised Standard Version (NRSV) unless otherwise noted.

5 The Hebrew term מְצֹרָע (*mazora*) is typically defined as leprosy in various translations of the Bible (e.g., NRSV, NIV, NAS, NKJV). However, the precise meaning is unclear. It appears that Naaman's skin condition or deformity does not hinder his military service or separate him from his troops and family.

6 Sidney Berman, "Greatness Versus Smallness: A Postcolonial Analysis of the Healing of Naaman (2 Kings 5), *Old Testament Essays* 29, no. 3 (2016): 409.

7 Julie F. Parker, *Valuable and Vulnerable: Children in the Hebrew Bible, Especially the Elisha Cycle* (Brown Judaic Studies, 2013), 161.

8 See also Deuteronomy 21:10–14; 1 Samuel 30:2.

9 Carolyn S. Leeb, *Away from the Father's House: The Social Location of the Na'ar and Na'arah in Ancient Israel* (Sheffield Academic Press, 2000), 126.

10 See Erik Erikson, *Identity and the Life Cycle* (Norton Press, 1994). Erikson's stages of psychosocial development include: Infancy: basic trust versus mistrust; Toddler: autonomy versus shame and doubt; Preschool-age: initiative versus guilt; School-age: industry versus inferiority; Adolescence: identity versus identity confusion; Young adulthood: intimacy versus isolation; Middle age: generativity versus stagnation; Older adulthood: integrity versus despair.

11 Cynthia R. Chapman, *The House of the Mother: The Social Roles of Maternal Kin in Biblical Hebrew Narrative and Poetry* (Yale University Press, 2016).

12 These generalizations about girls or women's agency are made regarding Israelite households with the recognition that the same may not be true for those considered foreigners or external to these households. See also, Jennie R Ebeling, *Women's Lives in Biblical Times* (T&T Clark, 2011).

13 Abram, later named Abraham, receives Egyptian slaves following his encounter with an Egyptian Pharoah in Genesis 12. Hagar features in Genesis 16.

14 See Walter Brueggemann, "2 Kings 5: Two Evangelists and a Saved Subject," *Missiology* 35, no. 3 (2007): 265.

15 De Andrado, "The Resilience of the Captive Girl Child in 2 Kings 5," 467.

16 De Andrado, "Resilience of the Captive," 468.

17 James C. Scott discusses how oppressed groups create a form of resistance in their conversations (hidden transcripts) that are unavailable to dominant groups. See Scott, *Domination and the Art of Resistance: Hidden Transcripts* (Yale University Press, 1992).

18 Jean Kyoung Kim, "Reading and Retelling Naaman's Story (2 Kings 5), *Journal for the Study of the Old Testament* 30, no. 1 (2005), 49–51, 53.

19 Robert Coles, *The Moral Intelligence of Children* (Random House, 1997), 5.

20 See Carol Meyers, *Rediscovering Eve: Ancient Israelite Women in Context* (Oxford University Press, 2013).

21 Meyers, *Rediscovering Eve*, 127.

22 Eduardo Bonilla-Silva and Victor Ray, "It's Real! Racism, Color Blindness, Obama, and the Urgent Need for Social Movement Politics," in *Crisis, Politics and Critical Sociology*, ed. Graham Cassano and Richard A. Dello-Buono (Brill, 2010) 47–48.

23 For more on the modern US militia movement see Catrina Doxsee, "Examining Extremism: The Militia Movement," *Center for Strategic and International Studies*, August 12, 2021, https://www.csis.org/blogs/examining-extremism/examining-extremism-militia-movement.

24 Bonilla-Silva and Ray, "It's Real! Racism, Color Blindness," 48.

25 Christopher Carlyle Clarke, "'Girls Play with Dolls and Boys Play with Soldiers': Examining Teachers and Parents' Gender Beliefs

and the Gender Identity of 8-10 Year Old Jamaican Boys," (PhD diss, University of Southern Florida, 2007), 15, https://digitalcommons.usf.edu/etd/180.

26 These groups are shaped by their geographical location, socio-economic status, religious background, education, familial structures, level of acculturation, cultural distinctiveness, etc.

27 Hyacinth Evans and Rose Davies, "Overview of Issues in Childhood Socialization in the Caribbean" in *Caribbean Families: Diversity Among Ethnic Groups*, ed. Jaipaul L. Roopnarine and Janet Brown (Greenwood Publishing Group, 1997), 14:5.

28 Ibid.

29 Ibid.

30 Barry Chevannes, Learning to Be a Man: Culture, Socialization, and Gender Identity in Five Caribbean Communities (University of West Indies Press, 2001), 43; see also: William Wedenoja and Diana Fox, "Jamaica," in *Encyclopedia of Sex and Gender: Men and Women in the World's Cultures*, ed. Carol R. Ember and Melvin Ember (Springer, 2003), 555–56

31 Janice A. McLean-Farrell, "'Ain't I a Child of God?': Gender and Christianity in Light of the Immigrant Experience," *Mission Studies* 31, no. 3 (2014): 366

32 McLean-Farrell, "Ain't I a Child of God?," 367.

33 Evans and Davies, "Overview of Issues in Childhood Socialization in the Caribbean," 6–7.

34 McLean-Farrell, "Ain't I a Child of God?," 370.

35 Janice McLean-Farrell, *West Indian Pentecostals: Living Their Faith in New York and London* (Bloomsbury, 2016).

36 That is being a law abiding, upstanding member of society, one who participates and demonstrates respectable behavior, avoids criminal activity, does well in school, is respectful of adults and elders, behaves in an orderly manner in public, etc.

37 Nancy Boyd-Franklin, *Black Families in Therapy: Understanding the African American Experience*, 2nd ed. (The Guilford Press, 2003), 90.

38 Desire Shenay Taylor, "The Impact of Racial Socialization and Racial Identity on Body Dissatisfaction in African American Women College Students" (PhD diss., University of Texas at Austin, 2015), 35.

39 Boyd-Franklin, *Black Families in Therapy*, 90.

40 Ibid.

41 Ibid.
42 A. Wade Boykin, "The Triple Quandary and the Schooling of Afro-American Children," in *The School Achievement of Minority Children: New Perspectives*, ed. Ulric Neisser (Routledge, 1986). https://doi.org/10.4324/9781315060187; see also A. Wade Boykin and Forrest D. Toms, "Black Child Socialization: A Conceptual Framework," in *Black Children: Social, Educational, and Parental Environments*, ed. Harriette Pipes McAdoo and John Lewis McAdoo (Sage, 1985), 31–51.
43 Taylor, "The Impact of Racial Socialization," 35.
44 Ibid.
45 Barrow, Christine, "Male Images of Women in Barbados," *Social and Economic Studies* 35, no. 3 (1986): 52.
46 McLean-Farrell, "Ain't I a Child of God?," 368.
47 Tamura Lomax, *Jezebel Unhinged: Loosing the Black Female Body in Religion & Culture* (Duke University Press, 2018), 49.
48 Ibid., 109.
49 Ibid.
50 Ibid.
51 See Emilie M. Townes, *Womanist Ethics and the Cultural Production of Evil* (Palgrave McMillan, 2006), 159.
52 Ta-Nehisi Coates, *Between the World and Me* (Spiegel and Grau, 2015), 10.
53 Townes, *Womanist Ethics and the Cultural Production of Evil*, 23.
54 Ibid., 21.
55 Ibid.
56 See Albert J. Raboteau, *Slave Religion: The "Invisible Institution" in the Antebellum South* (Oxford University Press, 2004).
57 Specific attention should be given the founding of the Baptist denomination by George Liele in 1784, the theological foundation and role church leaders in rebellions prior to emancipation and afterwards (Demerara Rebellion in Guyana in 1823, Baptist War Rebellion in 1831–32, and Morant Bay Rebellion in 1865), and the resilience of Black religion in providing alternative religious beliefs to a Christianity that demanded the denigration of Black personhood. These include: Kumina and Revivalism in Jamaica; Winti in Surinam; Shango in Trinidad and Grenada; and Kele in St. Lucia. For a discussion of interaction between these religious beliefs and Christianity, see Janice McLean-Farrell, *West Indian Pentecostals*, Chapter 1.

58 Emilie M. Townes, "Ethics as an Art of Doing the Work Our Souls Must Have," in *Womanist Theological Ethics: A Reader*, ed. Katie Geneva Cannon, Emilie M. Townes, and Angela Sims, (Westminster John Knox Press, 2011), 44.

59 Townes, "Ethics as an Art of Doing the Work Our Souls Must Have," 42.

60 Ibid., 43.

61 See Richard G. Tedeschi et al., eds., *Posttraumatic Growth: Positive Changes in the Aftermath of Crisis* (Routledge, 1998); Richard G. Tedeschi, and Lawrence G. Calhoun. "The Posttraumatic Growth Inventory: Measuring the Positive Legacy of Trauma," *Journal of Traumatic Stress* 9, no. 3 (1996): 455–71; Richard G. Tedeschi and Lawrence G. Calhoun, "Posttraumatic Growth: Conceptual Foundations and Empirical Evidence," *Psychological Inquiry* 15, no. 1 (2004): 1–18. http://www.jstor.org/stable/20447194; Robert A. Neimeyer, "Fostering Posttraumatic Growth: A Narrative Elaboration," *Psychological Inquiry* 15, no. 1 (2004): 53–59. http://www.jstor.org/stable/20447202.

62 Three exceptions are: Tabitha Grier-Reed et al., "Posttraumatic Growth and Flourishing in the Face of Racial Trauma," *Psychol Trauma* (2022); Emily E Manove et al., "Posttraumatic Growth in Low-Income Black Mothers Who Survived Hurricane Katrina," *American Journal of Orthopsychiatry* 89, no. 2 (2019): 144–58; Vinay Lal, "Unanchoring Islands: An Introduction to the Special Issue on 'Islands: Waterways, Flowways, Folkways,'" *Emergences: Journal for the Study of Media and Composite Cultures* 10, no. 2 (2000): 229–40, https://doi.org/10.1080/713665810.

63 Richelle B. White, *Daughters of Imani: A Christian Rites of Passage Program for African American Young Women* (Abington Press, 2005).

64 Marley Dias, *Marley Diaz Gets It Done: And So Can You!* (Scholastic Press, 2018).

65 "Sophie Cruz – Global Village Museum of Arts and Cultures," https://globalvillagemuseum.org/sophie-cruz/.

6

He Ain't Heavy, He's My Brother: Rereading Genesis 39–41 Through the Lens of Mass Incarceration

Raynard D. Smith

According to family psychologists, good parenting entails that all children in the family receive the same treatment indicating that they are equally loved.[1] This equal emotional distribution makes each child feel special and wanted. However, there are some situations in which parental-sibling favoritism exists and this can lead to the development of tension and resentment among siblings despite good parenting. The parental preference for a child who receives more attention, more affection, more privileges, and less discipline will not remain unnoticed by siblings. Parental choices in sibling priority can arouse negative emotions within the siblings that impact their sense of self, predispose them to depression, cause them to be more inclined to act aggressively, and diminish their academic performance.[2] Nowhere is this arousal of aggression and its consequences more evident than in the sibling rivalry evoked by favoritism that occurs in Genesis 37 between Joseph and his brothers.

In Genesis, we find the story of Joseph, the favorite son of Jacob, born to him by his favored wife, Rachel (Genesis 37:39–41).[3] As the favorite son among Jacob's twelve sons, Joseph finds himself the victim of a series of unfortunate events initiated by his jealous brothers, engendered in a family constellation in which Jacob shows special love for Joseph. "Jacob loved Joseph more than any of his other children because Joseph had been born to him in his old age . . . But his brothers hated Joseph because their father loved him more than the rest of them" (Genesis 37: 3–4).[4] While applying psychological concepts to biblical narratives is always risky at best, the family dynamics in Genesis warrant such a risk by exposing the possible effect of parental favoritism on unfavored children. In Genesis 37, the domino effect of Jacob's favoritism results in the brothers' attempt to take Joseph's life (37:26–27); Joseph becomes the object of human traffickers (37:28), then is enslaved to an Egyptian official, Potiphar (39:1), and subsequently is imprisoned due to the false accusations of attempted rape made by Potiphar's wife (39:7–20). Joseph's travails will ultimately end in his triumph as he becomes second-in-command to Pharoah, the most powerful person in Egypt. The trauma of these events potentially leaves a lasting effect on Joseph's psyche. However, no effect is more poignant than his experience of incarceration in Egypt, which easily could have spanned anywhere from seven to nine years.[5]

While he is incarcerated, Joseph's chances of reuniting with his family of origin are diminished but not impossible as the story will later bear out. Seemingly dispossessed of his father's love and the security of his home, Joseph's life is changed; he is forced to forge a new identity in which his past and present are at odds with one another. Joseph's story of imprisonment in Egypt can be instructional for contemporary conversations within Black churches regarding the mass incarceration of Black men, their experience as incarcerated persons, and their reentries to communities.[6] The high incidence of mass incarceration of Black males has taken its toll on individuals and their families as both become collateral damage in a system designed to profit from the exploitation of Black bodies.[7] Here, I offer some illustrations to interrogate the issue of mass incarceration and the prison industrial complex from biblical and psychological perspectives; this is done with the aim that increased awareness of the issue will lead to empathetic interventions with incarcerated persons and people who are returning to society, and will stimulate advocacy for equity in our criminal justice system.

A Dreamer, His Dreams, and His Destiny

We first encounter Joseph as a seventeen-year-old youth sent to help (or rather spy on) his brothers as they shepherd Jacob's flock (Genesis 37:2). In addition to the negative report that he provides to his father about his brothers, we are informed that Joseph is *loved* more than all of Jacob's other children (Genesis 37:3). Interestingly, it is not the negative report given to his father that disturbs his brothers, but rather the father's love for Joseph that provokes their ire. The text states, "But when his brothers saw that their father loved him more than all his brothers, they hated him, and could not speak peaceably to him" (Genesis 37:4). Miguel De La Torre surmises, "[Jacob] probably saw Joseph as the product of his true love; this would explain why he showered the boy with unhealthy attention."[8] However, their animosity is further kindled when Joseph asserts his importance and prestige by recounting to them his dreams. According to the text, "He said to them, 'Listen to this dream I dreamed. There we were binding sheaves in the field. Suddenly my sheaf rose and stood upright; then your sheaves gathered around it and bowed down to my sheaf. . . . so they hated him even more because of his dreams and his words" (Genesis 37: 6–8). This will not be the end of the young man's dreams. A subsequent dream will include even his parents paying obeisance to him (Genesis 37:9–10). While the father ponders the dream and its significance, the jealousy of the brothers grows; the dream ratchets up the jealousy that Shakespeare called "the green-eyed monster."[9] Kathleen O'Connor observes the intensified emotions that arise in the brothers based on the repetitive use of the word "hated" (37:4, 5, and 8).[10] This hatred derives from their jealousy of this favored son.

Jealousy as a motivating factor in this family's drama can be understood within the psychological dynamics of shame. The psychologist Mary Lamia states, "The potential disconnection experienced in jealousy often involves a social comparison. When you experience jealousy, you may assume that someone else is receiving the attention or adoration that you want for yourself. In some way, the other person appears more desirable."[11] This dynamic is observable in Joseph's interaction with his brothers and his father. Only Joseph, according to the text, receives a luxurious robe, a tunic with sleeves (cf. 2 Sam 13:18–19). This garment would not have been the standard attire for fieldwork and it draws attention to the likelihood that fieldwork was not Joseph's typical task within the family.[12] Miguel De La Torre asserts, "Besides tattling on his brothers, the outward expression of preference by Israel/Jacob demonstrated by the gift of the long-sleeve coat, and being excused from participating in hard work, Joseph further contributes to his brothers' ire by having dreams and being foolish enough to share them."[13] Lamia continues, "A response to jealousy that attacks others may result in aggressive and offensive behavior . . . aimed at breaking up the threatening liaison or re-establishing the primary relationship."[14] The brothers' decision to kill Joseph (37:20) sought to forever cut off the relationship between their father and the brother they despised. However, this plan is interrupted by the eldest brother, Reuben, who offers an alternative and seemingly less-lethal way of ridding themselves of Joseph. The text states, "But when Reuben heard it, he delivered him out of their hands, saying, 'let us not take his life.' . . . Shed no blood; throw him into this pit here in the wilderness, but lay no hand on him" (Genesis 37: 21–22). Does Reuben imagine that the pit would be any less perilous? What about death due to starvation and dehydration? O'Connor observes that, "The pit is empty and without water. So Joseph will not drown, but neither will he survive without water."[15] Judah's suggestion to sell Joseph, a profitable venture for the brothers, wins the day as he asks, "What profit is it if we kill our brother and conceal his blood?" (Genesis 37:26–28). The text is unclear as to whether the brothers can be implicated in selling Joseph since Midianite traders remove him from the pit and sell him to the Ishmaelites who take him to Egypt.[16] Nevertheless, it is their actions that place him in the pit to be sold. Upon learning of the apparent demise of Joseph, Jacob plunges into inconsolable grief (Genesis 37:34–35).

The narrative resumes in Genesis 39 where Joseph is purchased by Potiphar, "an officer of Pharaoh (Genesis 39:1).[17] In 39:2 through 39:5, the reader is given a theological lens by which to interpret all that follows.

The LORD was with Joseph, and he became a successful man; he was in the house of his Egyptian master. His master saw that the LORD was with him, and that the LORD caused all that he did to prosper in his hands. So Joseph found favor in his sight and attended him; he made him overseer of his house and put him in charge of all that he had. From the time that he made him overseer in his house and over all that he had, the LORD blessed the Egyptian's house for Joseph's sake; the blessing of the LORD was on all that he had, in house and field.

Despite the trusting relationship initially established between Joseph and Potiphar, Joseph still finds himself in a tenuous position as Potiphar's wife takes an unhealthy (i.e., lustful) interest in him (Genesis 39:7).[18] O'Connor asserts, "Her efforts to seduce him recur on a daily basis, and also on a daily basis Joseph refuses her."[19] In ancient Egyptian society one could be convicted for crimes against humanity (i.e., murder, adultery, or theft) or crimes against the Egyptian government or state. Crimes against the Egyptian government included treason, theft of public property, or a violation of religious institutions.[20] Joseph's unresponsiveness to her advances result in a false accusation of attempted rape that damages the bond forged between him and her husband, Potiphar. With the relationship now ruptured, an enraged Potiphar, trusting the words of his wife, casts Joseph into prison potentially subjecting him to harsh physical labor. (Genesis 39:19-20).[21]

From Favored Son, to Trusted Servant, to Incarcerated Felon

In prison, Joseph would encounter other prisoners (slaves) like himself who had not committed the crime for which they were allegedly convicted; in Egyptian society one was presumed guilty until proven innocent.[22] In this place of punitive confinement, Joseph has a fortuitous encounter with two of Pharaoh's servants—the baker and cupbearer—who have also become targets of Pharaoh's wrath (Genesis 40:1–3). Joseph is assigned to waiting on them, making them important, although still-fallen people in Pharaoh's cabinet (Genesis 40:4). The situation places Joseph by association near Pharaoh himself, despite his incarceration.[23] One can only imagine the depth of Joseph's fall from "grace" as the beloved son of his father, Jacob, to the despised Hebrew slave in the forced labor of the Egyptian empire. One can also sense his mental anguish knowing that his present circumstances are due in part to the initial betrayal of his brothers. Speculatively, Joseph's psychological state as a person unjustly incarcerated mirrors that of many prisoners today who are innocently convicted and imprisoned for crimes they did not commit.[24] Like Joseph, many African Americans males (and females) find themselves trapped in the prison industrial complex of the United States (a.k.a., the penal system) serving prison sentences that are disproportionately meted out, and in some cases, undeserved (i.e., the person was innocent). In the narrative, the fact that Joseph was not guilty of the claim of rape that led to his imprisonment could only add more insult to his already festering wounds.

Joseph, once the dreamer, now becomes the interpreter of dreams when the baker and cupbearer have a series of troubling night visions (Genesis 40:5–6, 9–11, 16–17). Joseph's ability to interpret their dreams does not receive the negative response he had received from his brothers. Joseph manages to initiate a bond with these prisoners, who may in some sense replace his brothers and the family he no longer has. In a modern context, the prison subculture and socialization process create a new "family" designed to protect and sustain inmates until they are either paroled or die in prison. Newly imprisoned inmates undergo a process of *prisonization* in which they internalize the ways, rules, and behaviors of the prison subculture.[25] The Genesis text does not depict the relational aspects of Egyptian prisoners. However, is it possible that Joseph uses his ability to interpret dreams to ensure his survival among the other prisoners?

As Joseph's interpretations come to fruition (the cupbearer is restored to Pharaoh's service, while the baker is executed), his renderings seem to accomplish two things: they solidify his relationship with the cupbearer, and position him for an encounter with Pharaoh, his warden. Joseph presumes that his aid to the cupbearer has strengthened their relationship such that he asks the cupbearer to speak on his behalf to Pharaoh. "But please remember me when everything is going well for you, and please be kind enough to mention me to the king and help me get out of this prison. After all, I was kidnapped from the land of the Hebrews, and even here in Egypt I didn't do anything to deserve being put in prison" (Genesis 40: 14–15). In making this request, one hears Joseph's continued protestation of his innocence. However, once released, the cupbearer resumes his normal role in Pharaoh's service, seemingly forgetting Joseph, leaving him to languish in prison (Genesis 40:21, 23). This selective forgetting may suggest the cupbearer's own desire to distance himself from the traumatic experience of prison and those in it, including Joseph.

In our contemporary time, as a form of control, inmates once released from incarceration are forbidden by the penal system to consort with former associates (those still in prison or those persons known prior to incarceration). When most offenders are released back to society, contact with former cell mate(s) is restricted since prisoners are prohibited from receiving phone calls. Unless the returning citizen gives the prisoner his other contact information, contact with the fellow prison mate is impossible. Unless or until the remaining prisoner initiates contact—since there is no restriction on who the prisoner can call barring contact with journalists—the continuity of the relationship becomes nearly nonexistent.[26] In this respect, the experience of Joseph losing contact with the cupbearer, and having to rely on the cupbearer to establish contact, would resonate with the experience of many African American males whose contact with their former prison mates is curtailed once that other person is released. For Joseph, two years lapse before his prospect of being released materializes.

Eventually, the cupbearer recollects his encounter with Joseph, not because of friendship but rather to curry favor with Pharaoh (Genesis 41:1). It is not until Pharaoh experiences disturbing dreams himself and is in need of an interpreter (no one in his kingdom can help) that the cupbearer remembers Joseph (Genesis 41:1–8). The cupbearer mentions the young Hebrew who correctly interpreted his dreams and the dreams of the deceased baker while in prison (Genesis 41:9–13). One imagines the sense of urgency as Joseph is summoned from prison to perform a similar interpretative task for Pharaoh (Genesis 41:14). According to Anita Stratos,

> Ancient Egyptians used the messages in their dreams to cure illnesses, make important State decisions, and even to decide where to build a temple or when to wage a battle. Dreams were divine predictions of the future. They were messages from the gods that could be foretelling of impending disasters or, conversely, of good fortune; therefore, understanding the significance of ones' dreams was an important part of the culture.[27]

This ability to interpret dreams proved to be advantageous for Joseph because he had the gift of dream interpretation which surpassed the skills of Pharaoh's court magicians.

Joseph's interpretation of Pharaoh's dreams saves Pharaoh and his kingdom from famine and secures Joseph's release and promotion when Pharaoh announces, "Since God has shown you all this, there is no one so discerning and wise as you. You shall be over my house, and all my people shall order themselves as you command: only with regard to the throne will I be greater than you" (Genesis 41: 39-40).

Despite the challenges he encountered, Joseph, an imprisoned Hebrew slave, becomes the viceroy, the second-in-command of Egypt. For Joseph, his newly found freedom, status, and position is a long way from his pit experience and the animosity of his brothers. Now a contributing member to the Egyptian economy, Joseph's strategic plan directly impacts the survivability of communities affected by the famine.[28] Joseph's return to society proved to be a blessing to Pharaoh and the Egyptian people. His wisdom and administrative skills helped to stave off disaster for Egypt. Contemporarily, most inmates who are incarcerated express a hopeful glimpse of themselves contributing to their families upon being released. According to the Brookings Working Group of Prison Reform,

In surveys and interviews with men and women in prison, the majority express hope for their future. Most were employed before their incarceration and have family that will help them get back on their feet. Many have children that they were supporting and want to reconnect with. They realize that finding a job may be hard, but they believe they will be able to avoid the actions that got them into trouble, principally committing crimes and using illegal substances.[29]

Their analysis counters the argument that incarceration has the tendency to deform the personality of an individual, which leads to a life of ongoing criminality. The conclusions of the Brookings Group indicate that not all experiences of incarceration produce social deviants. When applied to Joseph's situation, his reentry and contribution to society clearly demonstrates the absence of a criminal mentality. Joseph's release from Egypt's prison system prefigures that of Nelson Mandela who was a political prisoner in South Africa under the apartheid regime. Upon Mandela's release in 1990 he would rise to become the president of South Africa in 1994, a contributing citizen who led South Africans into a peaceful political transfer of power.[30]

Family Dynamics - Returning Citizen

Meanwhile, the situation in Canaan has not been so prosperous for Joseph's family. A famine hits the entire region bringing to fruition Pharoah's nightmares (Genesis 41:53–57). Jacob hears of food in Egypt and sends his sons to secure enough grain for the family (and livestock) to survive the drought (Genesis 42: 1–2). Upon arrival in Egypt, the sons seek to procure grain from the viceroy, who unbeknownst to them was the brother they sold into slavery as a young lad just seventeen years old (Genesis 37:2). Joseph's dream of his family paying homage to him comes true. "And Joseph's brothers came and bowed themselves before him with their faces to the ground" (Genesis 42:6). Immediately, Joseph recognizes these ten "strangers" as his estranged brothers—a recognition that is not yet obvious to them—and prompts his harsh response (Genesis 42:7, 8). Does seeing and hearing the voices of his siblings trigger Joseph's memories and the pain of separation from his family? Does he momentarily experience flashbacks to his years of unjust incarceration and the animosity of the brothers who set him on that path?

Joseph had been separated from his brothers for approximately twenty-two years, but when his brothers arrive in Egypt and are brought into his presence to purchase grain, his memory is immediately jarred. The text states he instantly recognizes his brothers. Perhaps his recollection prompts him to accuse them of espionage; he charges them of seeking Egypt's vulnerabilities (Genesis 42:9). Joseph's initial response to these presumed strangers displays his distrust of his siblings. Does his behavior unintentionally reveal some unresolved anger at their betrayal? Is he now presented with an opportunity to even the score? While the brothers do not spend years in prison, they now know what it means to be among the imprisoned for three days (Genesis 42:10–17). The prison experience can have either a positive or negative outcome. When the transformation is positive, it can help reorient the individual to the important things in life. A person can emerge from this experience with a renewed determination to stay free. When the transformation is negative, it can lead to further downward spiraling and social dislocation. Joseph's imprisonment, subsequent elevation, and assimilation into Egyptian society have changed him (physically, socially, and psychologically) such that his brothers do not recognize him.

Confinement, isolation, and separation from society can bring about a real encounter with one's own conscience. It can create space and time in which one has the opportunity to examine one's life and make conscious decisions to change or remain the same. In prison, the brothers have this existential encounter, which possibly unleashes their hidden guilty consciences. They interpret their experience as divine retribution, "Alas, we are paying the penalty for what we did to our brother; we saw his anguish when he pleaded with us, but we would not listen. That is why this anguish has come upon us" (Genesis 42: 21). As they quarrel in their native tongue, Joseph understands their words and privately weeps (Genesis 42: 23–24). How should we interpret Joseph's tears? What underlying emotions do they reveal? On the one hand, he could be concluding that their attitudes and motives remain unchanged from their youth as they fail to take responsibility for their actions; Joseph still does not matter to them. On the other hand, the brothers' presence and behaviors might be re-evoking his thoughts and feelings. Their actions have emotionally and physically separated him from his beloved father and brother, Benjamin. Both explanations appear at work here. Joseph requires proof of their transformation, a clear indication that he remains highly suspicious of them and their motives. Unconvinced, he proposes that they prove him wrong by exchanging one brother for another.

> 30 "The man who is governor of the land spoke very
> harshly to us," they told him. "He accused us of being spies
> scouting the land. 31 But we said, 'We are honest men, not
> spies. 32 We are twelve brothers, sons of one father. One
> brother is no longer with us, and the youngest is at home
> with our father in the land of Canaan.' 33 Then the man
> who is governor of the land told us, 'This is how I will find
> out if you are honest men. Leave one of your brothers here
> with me, and take grain for your starving families and go
> on home. 34 But you must bring your youngest brother
> back to me. Then I will know you are honest men and not
> spies. Then I will give you back your brother, and you may
> trade freely in the land.' (Genesis 42:30–34)

Joseph's request that one brother (Simeon) replace another brother (Benjamin) would prove their honest intentions. But what of Joseph's intentions? In making his brothers appear as spies, does he still carry the sting of their rejection and betrayal?

Meanwhile, in Canaan, Jacob still mourns the loss of Rachel and Joseph. The brothers' proposition to take her remaining son, Benjamin, is more than he can bear (Genesis 42:36–38). Nevertheless, due to the persistence of the famine and the survival needs of the family, Jacob submits to their request, albeit with deep reservations. But, perhaps in resignation and sorrow, Jacob prepares a generous offering to send to the viceroy (Joseph) and allows the brothers to take Benjamin with them stating, "may God Almighty grant you mercy before the man, so that he may send back your other brother and Benjamin" (Genesis 43:14). Then, with their father's blessing that entrusts them to the providential care of El Shaddai, the brothers return to Egypt with their youngest brother in tow.

For the families of the incarcerated, life continues; but, not without adjustments. Depending on the incarcerated person's role in the family, these adjustments range from minor to major changes (physical, emotional, and financial).[31] Their loss of role within the family due to incarceration may threaten the emotional bonds of attachment and engender grief reactions within family members. The absence of men to incarceration could predispose families to economic instability, children and relatives to emotional turmoil, and communities to social deprivation.

Restoring Families

One can imagine the long journey from Canaan to Egypt. While Joseph's suspicions about his brothers have been abated, the brothers return to Egypt a bit more cautiously this time (Genesis 43:18–22). When the brothers meet Joseph, they bow before him, reminiscent of his dream (Genesis 43:26). A feast is prepared in their honor as Joseph asks about the well-being of their father, weeping privately once again upon seeing Benjamin (Genesis 43:30). Despite the reunion, Joseph and his brothers do not eat together as a family.[32] The separation maintains Joseph's assimilated identity as an Egyptian since he has not revealed his familial connections to them. During the meal, Benjamin's servings are five times that of his brothers and no brother questions this obvious favoritism (43:34). All seems well as they drank and were merry with him. But is all well? Joseph puts before the brothers one final test that will determine if they have truly changed for the better. As the brothers get ready to return to Canaan, Joseph's servant is instructed to fill Benjamin's sack with Joseph's personal silver cup used for divination (Genesis 44:15). This act of sabotage suggests that he is still suspicious of his brothers' motives.

Upon the instructions from Joseph, his servant follows the brothers as they return to Canaan. He stops them and accuses them of theft, an accusation that initiates a search through their belongings. Joseph's sacred cup is discovered in Benjamin's sack. He pronounces judgment upon Benjamin condemning him to become his slave. Judah intervenes and offers to take his brother's place. Judah intends to keep his promise to Jacob at all costs. He understands the detrimental emotional effect that failing to return with Benjamin will cause his father and the entire family (Genesis 44:18–34). Although somewhat different, there are stories of older brothers, whose lives have become entangled with the criminal justice system who, as a result, become cautionary examples for younger family members to discourage them from following a similar path.

Judah's genuine concern for his family elicits Joseph's emotional visceral reaction. "Then Joseph could no longer control himself before all those who stood by him, and he cried out, 'send everyone away from me'" (Genesis 45:1). Left alone with his brothers, he reveals his true identity. "I am your brother, Joseph, whom you sold into Egypt" (Genesis 45: 4). Upon revealing his true identity to his long-estranged brothers, Joseph exhibits a spirit of humility and forgiveness. The emotional bond that appeared to be forever severed when he was first sold into captivity re-emerges and perhaps is stronger than before. The story concludes with all the family (including Jacob) relocating to Egypt, where they are cared for by Joseph, who reassures them that their experiences were divinely orchestrated, "Even though you intended to do harm to me, God intended it for good, in order to preserve a numerous people" (Genesis 50:20).

The Impact of Mass Incarceration upon the Black Family

When we juxtapose the biblical narrative of Joseph and his family with the modern-day experiences of imprisoned Black males and their families, we find numerous similarities: the grieving experienced by both the prisoner and his family—upon, during, and after his incarceration; the dealing with the prison subculture that tends to alter the psyche for the purpose of survival; the navigating of stigma at being socially outcast; the negotiating new social and economic statuses; the living with inadequate financial resources to make ends meet; and, the devaluing of humanness as a result of the prison experience. Herein, we will explore these major issues that face our imprisoned Black males and their families, and offer solution-based interventions for those returning to mainstream society.

Just as Joseph upon being released from prison and placed over Egypt's food preservation project proved to be useful to the survival of his family and the Ancient Near East, so too are Black males (and females) who have been incarcerated, and who will be returning home. Their complete restoration to their families and the Black community is vital to the healthy continuity of family and community life. But will Black churches be willing and ready to receive them, providing them with the support that they need to successfully reacclimate themselves to mainstream society? First, a glimpse of the magnitude of the issue of incarceration in America is telling.

America imprisons its people at the highest rate of any country.[33] The vast majority of these people will be returning to society. A statement from the United States Department of Justice explains:

Over 10,000 ex-prisoners are released from America's state and federal prisons every week and arrive on the doorsteps of our nation's communities. More than 650,000 ex-offenders are released from prison every year, and studies show that approximately two-thirds will likely be rearrested within three years of release. The high volume of returnees is a reflection on the tremendous growth in the U.S. prison population during the past 30 years. For the communities to which most former prisoners return (communities which are often impoverished and disenfranchised neighborhoods with few social supports and persistently high crime rates), the release of ex-offenders represents a variety of challenges.[34]

Here are the facts of what we know about families affected by incarceration: According to the Family History of Incarceration Survey (FamHIS) conducted in 2018, nearly half of the population has had a close family member caught up in the throes of the US criminal justice system.[35] Of those racial and ethnic groups who had a close family member tied to the US penal system, African Americans rated the highest percentage at 63 percent, followed by Latinx at 48 percent, trailed by whites at 42 percent.[36] Of male prisoners, 47 percent are fathers of children under the age of eighteen.[37] Yet, a higher percentage of female prisoners, 58 percent, are mothers who have minor children either left to the care of a relative or in the foster care system.[38] It is estimated that, at any given time, 5.8 million children have a parent who is or has been incarcerated.[39] Veronica Crawford Lynch contends that prior to incarceration the majority of these individuals "were caring and in the lives of their children."[40]

When parents become incarcerated, their absence from the home and the life of their children causes financial, social, psychological, and spiritual disruptions for the family. It impacts the bonds of attachments that exist between mothers, fathers, and their children, creating the possibility of "psychological stress, antisocial behavior, academic suspension or expulsion, economic hardship, and criminal activity."[41]

Like Joseph sold into slavery and imprisoned in Egypt, the mass incarceration of African American males has caused them to be absent from their families and has directly impacted the stability of the Black family and Black community. One in every six Black males between the ages of twenty-five and fifty-four has disappeared from the daily life of their families.[42] Their absence challenges the fragile emotional bonds of attachment that connect them to their families, friends, significant others, and loved ones.

The bond of attachment plays a significant role in causing these males as well as their family members to suffer and experience sadness attributed to the loss. Social psychologist John Bowlby's work on attachment theory is helpful in understanding the lived experiences of incarcerated African American males and their families. Bowlby defines attachment as a "lasting psychological connectedness between human beings."[43] He contends that children are born into the world with an innate predisposition to form an emotional bond with their primary caregiver—usually their mother. This emotional attachment shields them from the overwhelming anxiety of being alone in the vast universe; it is derived from a need for security and survival. The attachment formed among the primary caregiver–child dyad helps the child to establish a secure base from which they can begin to launch and explore the social field. It is from this initial attachment relationship that all later bonds are formed, thus contributing to the psychological and emotional well-being and security of the child and future adult in the social field. A threat or disruption to this bond of attachment can cause the child to experience extreme anxiety known as separation anxiety.

When African American males become entangled with the criminal justice system, family members experience a threat to their bond of affection toward the individual. Many family members suffer in silence. Pastoral psychologist Wayne Oates talks about how family members, especially parents, experience what he identifies as "disenfranchised grief" while their child is away in prison.[44] The hopes, dreams, and aspirations that they had for their child are dissolved, or at least put on hold, as they become embroiled in the penal system. Many have no place to process their grief since there is such a stigma and shame attached to one's family member being in prison. Many come to church Sunday after Sunday with a grieving heart but suffer in silence due to the stigma attached to having a family member incarcerated, fearing what others might think about them.

Often overlooked when Black males are incarcerated is the collateral damage to the family. Their separation from their significant others and children directly affects their emotional and spiritual well-being. According to social science analyst Eric Martin, children whose parents are involved in the criminal justice system are prone to suffer from psychological strain, antisocial behavior, suspension or expulsion from school, and economic hardship; they are six times more likely to be involved in criminal activity.[45] Partners of incarcerated individuals suffer from depression and economic hardship being deprived of the income that the incarcerated spouse or significant other might have contributed to the overall financial stability of the family. Awareness of the ways in which incarceration of Black males affects their relationships presents an opportunity for Black churches to intervene.

Pastoral Care Opportunities for the Black Churches to Black Families of the Incarcerated

In the introduction of their edited volume, *Ministry with Prisoners & Families: The Way Forward*, W. Wilson Goode and his co-editors make the following observation to the Black churches:

> There is a crisis in our criminal justice system today, a crisis African Americans churches must not ignore. We see the crisis of millions of lives in our communities that are affected by crime and the justice system. We experience it in the disproportionate number of African Americans currently incarcerated in our nations' jails and prison. The crisis swells as we consider the numbers of children, spouses, mothers, fathers, sisters, brothers, and significant others left behind to deal with grief, anger, separation, and shame.[46]

Here there is a clarion call for Black churches to become involved in offering pastoral interventions that directly support those who are or have been impacted by the criminal justice system—the incarcerated individual and the family as well. The incarceration of one individual has rippling effects upon the Black family and Black community. Veronica Crawford Lynch contends that Black churches have a missional mandate to address the needs of those who are affected by incarceration. This mandate is found in Matthew 25: 34–39 where Jesus talks about providing food for the hungry, care for the sick, and visitation to the imprisoned. Keith Reeves in his article, "Finding a Lazarus" identifies the Black churches as being a significant resource and force in countering the scourge of mass incarceration of Black males noting the number of Black churches that exist in America:

> With an estimated 50,000 black churches (including quite a number of wealthy, dynamic, and influential megachurches) and millions of congregants, there is reason to believe that black religious institutions can

> make a meaningful difference. The operative question is not so much what 'the black church' will ultimately do or not do, but what role, exactly, it will play in raising the life trajectories of dispirited young black men and their families and children (the vast number of whom are left with deeper emotional and financial scars). Nothing less than the comprehensive and concerted engagement of the black church holds any promise of significant success.[47]

Placing the responsibility on Black churches, these authors highlight key areas where congregations can become more deeply involved in the lives of African American males and their families. This engagement goes beyond the traditional prison ministry model of simply visiting correctional facilities for worship services or Bible studies. Instead, they advocate for more comprehensive and proactive strategies that address the broader needs of incarcerated or returning Black men, as well as their families. These holistic approaches are designed to support not only the transformation of individuals but also the restoration and strengthening of their family units.

Lynch, in her article "Facilitating Connectedness between Families and Incarcerated Individuals," outlines a myriad of ways in which Black churches can serve as bridges that seek to help families maintain contact with their family member while they are in prison.[48] While mainly focused on children maintaining contact with their incarcerated parents, I have extended her ideas to encompass children having access to any incarcerated member of their family. Lynch rightly asserts that the first step is for churches to educate themselves about the overall criminal justice system and how it impacts public policy and mental health outcomes, economic stability, and child welfare for families.[49] She delineates a list of six initiatives that churches can provide in support of efforts to maintain the relationships of family members with their beloved incarcerated member.

First, Black churches can collaborate with already existing programs that seek to keep families in contact with their imprisoned family members. This would call for the leadership taking the initiative to explore what community agencies are available to provide services supporting families in maintaining contact with their imprisoned family member.[50]

Second, churches can draw upon the expertise and experience of those members in their congregations who are clinical mental health professionals to provide free counseling to family members who may need to talk with someone about their feelings of having a family member in prison. As mentioned above, many people who have a family member in prison suffer in silence. They fear that knowledge of their son (or daughter) being in prison will bring shame to their name within the community of faith. Having designated members who are proficient in mental health counseling, set aside in your church to whom family members can go anonymously, can prove to be a tremendous asset. It can create a safe space that allows those who are affected by having a loved one in prison a place to go to share their burden of what pastoral psychologist Wayne Oates identifies as "disenfranchised sorrow."[51]

Third, collaborate with prison chaplains and other prison administrators in developing a system that eliminates existing barriers that inhibit maintaining relationships between incarcerated persons and their family members. The penal system can strip the inmate of his or her identity as a father (or mother) and this challenges the bond of affection that may exist with their children. There will need to be an intentional effort to remind incarcerated individuals of their important familial roles, and help cultivate their parental identities.

Fourth, advocate for family-friendly visiting areas and time schedules which promote the frequency of families visiting their incarcerated family member. Here, Black churches can serve as advocates for the creation of family-friendly environments within the prison that will be less threatening to adults and children visiting their loved one.

Fifth, emphasize the primacy of the parenting and caregiver role when designing community outreach programs. This can particularly be of importance when holidays come. Through initiatives of the church, prisoners can maintain their contact with their outside family members remembering them at gift-giving time. One such agency is Angel Tree which is a ministry of Prison Fellowship located throughout the US. Its ministry consists of local congregation members who volunteer to purchase and deliver gifts to children in the name of their prisoner-parent.[52] Black churches can collaborate with Angel Tree to provide services to families who have a family member who is incarcerated.

And sixth, interact with parents and the legal justice system to ensure that the rights of family members are not terminated prematurely. In this role Black churches can hold the prison system accountable to the family while also serving as a buffer and supporter to the imprisoned family member, helping them to process their feelings and emotions.

In addition, Lynch proposes that Black churches can "develop partnerships with either media outlets or libraries to set up high speed videoconferencing so that [family members] can connect with their loved ones through the Internet," collaborate with government agencies in the provision of temporary housing for formerly incarcerated persons and their families, and develop a summer camp program or retreat for families of incarcerated people—programs that are strictly designed to address their emotional, psychological and spiritual needs.[53] Her ideas are wonderful strategies in which Black churches can play a role in bridging the gap between family members and those who are incarcerated.

Pastoral Care Opportunities for the Black Churches to African American Returning Citizens

While Lynch's focus is mainly on helping children of family members who are incarcerated mitigate the trauma of having a family member incarcerated, Harold Dean Trulear focuses on how Black churches can directly provide support to Black males who are incarcerated and returning citizens.[54] He offers effective suggestions for ways in which Black churches can be of support to Black males (and Black females as well) who are seeking to be reintegrated into society. He calls on leaders in the Black churches to seek to create an environment that is welcoming and affirming of returning citizens by suggesting that Black churches need to become "healing communities" that normalize their outreach to those caught up in the criminal justice system.[55] He asserts that the Healing Communities model seeks to engage congregations in restoration and healing. People in their congregations affected by crime, incarceration, and reintegration are restored by transforming hearts and minds, creating a sense of welcome inclusion, reducing stigma and shame, and building networks of support that start in houses of worship and expand to transform the community at large.[56] With this mindset, he calls upon Black churches to consider their outreach to this population just as they would be concerned about those who are sick, in need of hospital visitation, and the ongoing pastoral support of the clergy and congregation. He poses the question,

> What would it look like if congregations began responding to incarceration in the same way we respond to hospitalizations? In times of illness and even death, every congregation marshalls its resources to care for the individuals and families affected. Jesus mentions our faithful response to both incarceration and illness as two marks of the believing church (Matthew 25: 31–46). Why do we view responding to illness as the business of the entire congregation, while outreach to the imprisoned is the responsibility of a specialized, often marginalized, ministry team?[57]

In advocating this response, Trulear espouses a new model for ministry with those who are incarcerated that is more encompassing than the traditional model of the prison ministry team. He advocates for a reentry model that is led by the leader of the Black churches with the whole congregation becoming engaged in the effort to radically address the needs of the incarcerated returning citizens and their families. With this model there is a call for a change in the culture, making prison ministry and reentry central to the overall mission of the church thus making these churches what he calls Stations of Hope. To destigmatize the issue of incarceration, He suggests that Black church leaders incorporate the issue of incarceration in their Sunday worship, altar prayers, and sermons, and organize Bible studies around the theme of incarceration. He notes that as the starting point in the work of prison ministry and reentry, Black churches can begin this initiative with their own members who may have a loved one incarcerated. He states, "Beginning with families in their own congregations, houses of worship can provide ministries of restoration and healing through their existing assets: acceptance, love, caring, forgiveness, reconciliation, redemption, and restoration can occur."[58] Here congregations would mobilize their resources of support upon the initial arrest of a family member's child, within their congregation, and extend their assistance throughout the imprisonment into the period of reentry helping the person to become reintegrated into society. This will call for an attitudinal change where they first begin by assuming a posture of nonjudgment and positive regard for those who are involved in the criminal justice system. That is the first step needed to establish a "healing relationship" with the incarcerated individual and/or his family.

In the narrative, Joseph forgave his brothers who had cruelly inflicted an atrocious act, selling him into slavery and causing him several years of agony and separation from his father and family. Like Joseph, there are untold thousands of Black males who are or have been incarcerated while maintaining their innocence. They have been wrongly convicted by the criminal justice system of a crime they did not commit. For these individuals the idea of forgiveness may not come so easily. The wrong that has been done to them, its collateral damage—loss of job, loss of family contact, loss of social status—and the profound sense of shame may have filled them with anger and bitterness. They will need to be given space and time to process the damage that has been done to their lives. Empathy from Black churches can play a major role in this process. For those victimized by the criminal justice system, to be fully free from the past hurt and pain inflicted on them, forgiveness is the way to restoration. Here I draw upon Al Miles's definition of forgiveness. He contends, "Forgiveness is the decision on the part of a person who has been abused, betrayed, or wronged to let go of or put aside the justifiable anger, bitterness, and hurt that arises from being victimized."[59] Black churches must be willing to walk alongside these men on their path of healing and restoration providing them with empathetic pastoral care and counseling. While supporting the individual journey of forgiveness, Black churches can also work toward systemic change. By advocating for criminal justice reform and partnering with organizations that fight for the rights of the wrongfully incarcerated, Black churches can help prevent others from enduring a similar injustice.

Becoming a Healing Community: A Station of Hope

Trulear, in his text *Healing Communities USA Training Guide*, defines a Healing Community as a station of hope, a "congregation where redemption values, reconciliation, forgiveness, and love replace the shame and stigma of crime and incarceration. It doesn't justify criminalized behavior, but it does recognize that all people are created in God's image and worthy of dignity and respect."[60] He advocates that those congregational members who will participate in the Healing Communities become familiar with the criminal justice system in their community. This could be done by engaging the theme of incarceration in a Bible study format and then inviting in guest speakers to address the congregation on the particular criminal justice issues that they will need to know in order to do informed ministry to people who have been incarcerated.

Trulear's model outlines a series of steps which leaders of Black churches can take in order to establish a significant relationship with persons who are accused or convicted of crime.

From the outset, leaders need to attempt to make contact with people as early as possible, either upon their being accused or convicted. This can be accomplished by churches including announcements informing their church membership that when someone in their family or themselves is arrested they are encouraged to contact the pastor just as they would inform the pastor of someone who was sick or going for a surgical procedure in their family. The pastor will then offer to meet with them to discuss the details of their arrest but most importantly to begin the church's support of them as they journey through the criminal justice system. During Sunday morning service, the congregation will be informed of the situation and prayer for the individual and all parties involved will be offered. Information concerning the person who is incarcerated can be placed on the public bulletin board where the general membership can view it and, in their own manner and through appropriate ways, seek to provide support. Trulear asserts, "Starting the engagement with an individual upon his or her arrest is important because that is when fear and trembling are most stark and the need for support the greatest. The relationship formed at that point can be built upon and deepened as the person moves through the criminal justice process-to prison and (in most cases) the eventual return home."[61]

Members are encouraged to continue contact with the person who is incarcerated through writing letters, sending cards during significant events in the person's life (like birthdays, anniversaries, and holidays), making telephone calls, sending emails (using the Federal Bureau of Prisons system), and visiting the person. Trulear contends that consistent contact with individuals who are incarcerated communicates positive support and can be a deciding factor in the person's reentry once released. "We know that the more contact an individual has with positive support during incarcerations, the more likely they are to be successful in their reentry. More contact, more success."[62]

Congregations will need to be made aware of the regulations surrounding letter writing, phone calls, and visitation. This information can often be found on the website of the penal institution or by contacting the prison's chaplaincy department. Yet beyond the traditional prison ministry model, the Healing Communities model encourages congregations to a greater level of involvement by attending the incarcerated individual's court appearances. If there is a lawyer in one's congregation, they can be solicited to assist in the person's defense. Or the congregation can make contact with an attorney through its own networks of contacts. Members can also help with identifying witnesses to testify in court on behalf of their incarcerated individual.[63]

These initiatives are undergirded by the fact that the accused individual takes full responsibility for their actions and behaviors and is truly repentant for whatever they may have done. Trulear states, "Redemption requires accountability, and for those who will be coming home from prison one day, accountability is the first step toward successful reintegration. To be accountable, one must acknowledge the wounded (the victim, family, and community). Restoration does not negate restitution."[64] Just as Joseph forgave his brothers in order for complete healing to take place, healing communities and congregations must be prepared to offer forgiveness to the individual and also to encourage the individual to forgive themself.[65] Furthermore, sermons and Bible studies which focus on the theme of forgiveness and reconciliation can prove useful in helping congregation members to create a nonjudgmental environment where attitudes of forgiveness abound. Healing Communities must take an active role in guiding the individual both while inside the penal institution and outside to making appropriate contact with professional and volunteer supportive resources such as education (GED programs), job training, and mental health and substance abuse treatment centers.[66]

With the network of support that Trulear espouses, people who are incarcerated and seeking to become reacclimated to society will have a better chance of succeeding. Relationships with vital supportive individuals will have already been made while inside. Once outside, these relationships would simply continue as mentoring-like relationships where the returning citizen would feel completely supported and the goal of becoming reacclimated to society would become a communal endeavor.

Conclusion

While for Joseph this narrative is part of a larger divine plan (Genesis 45:5; 50:20), for Black males caught up in the US criminal justice system it is mostly the outcome of unjust and oppressive systems that target minority communities, in particular the Black community. The war on drugs and the influx of harsher sentencing laws in the 1980s and 1990s have created a situation where a disproportionate number of Black males have become entangled in the US criminal justice system. Raphael Warnock boldly asserts, "In some ways, one might well argue that America's current system of disproportionately policing, targeting, sentencing, and stigmatizing scores of Black people in its so-called War on Drugs is as dehumanizing and destructive as slavery itself."[67] Since 1990, more than 1.1 million prisoners (both male and female) have been imprisoned for low-level or non-violent crimes. This has resulted in the fact that almost half of state prisoners are convicted of non-violent crimes, and more than half of federal prisoners are serving time for drug offenses.[68] Because this scourge of mass incarceration has disproportionately affected Black males and the Black community, there is a need for Black churches to take an active role in seeking to repair the breach.

Mass incarceration has ravaged the lives of millions of Black males and has ripple effects upon their parents, partners, children, and other significant individuals in their lives. Within one year's time, it is estimated that 650,000 incarcerated persons will be released back to society. The US Bureau of Justice statistics estimates that two-thirds of those who are released will be rearrested within a year.[69] The rate of recidivism is high. However, the Black Church's engagement in ministries and efforts—like Healing Communities advocated by Trulear—can reduce the rate of recidivism. It can provide those seeking to reacclimate themselves to society with a safe harbor in which they can be sheltered from the onslaught of the criminal justice system and the stigma attached to it that seeks to forever humiliate them and cause them to be what Gregory Ellison calls "social junk."[70] With Black congregations making this population of Black males as the central focus of their "evangelical thrust" where forgiveness, redemption, and reconciliation take precedence, there can be greater salvaging of Black males from the effects of the dehumanizing institution of the US penal system. For the Black churches to assume this posture of forgiveness, redemption, and reconciliation is to recognize that our Black males (and sisters) caught up in the criminal justice system truly are not heavy, they are our brothers.[71]

Questions for Discussion and Further Reflection

- Throughout the Joseph narrative, the narrator is weaving the theme that during Joseph's many disappointments God was with him. What evidence do you see in the narrative that God's hand was at work in Joseph's life? And how might this speak to us today?

- How does your congregation address the needs of its sick and shut-in members and how might this translate into your congregation's outreach to those who are caught up in the US penal system?

- What are some of the distinctions between addressing the needs of those who are sick and shut-in, and addressing the needs of those who are incarcerated?

- What resources do your congregations already have in place that could be mobilized to serve those who are caught up in the US penal system? What would these interventions look like and how would they be implemented?

Additional Resources:

"What Shall We Then Do?: A Family Freedom Kit," The Annie E. Casey Foundation.

The New Jim Crow Study Guide and Call to Action, Samuel DeWitt Proctor Conference (CreateSpace Independent Publishing, 2016).

Richard A. Mendel, *No Place for Kids: The Case for Reducing Juvenile Incarceration*. The Annie E. Casey Foundation, October 4, 2011, https://www.aecf.org/resources/no-place-for-kids-full-report.

Kirsten Weir, "Life on the Outside," *Monitor on Psychology* 26, no. 11 (2015).

Endnotes

1 See Ilan Shrira, "When Parents Play Favorites," Psychology Today, January 10, 2009, https://www.psychologytoday.com/us/blog/the-narcissus-in-all-us/200901/when-parents-play-favorites.

2 Shrira, "When Parents Play Favorites."

3 See Chapter 1, "The Mourning After: Leah, Loss and Depression in Genesis 29."

4 All translations are based on the New Living Translation unless otherwise noted.

5 Joseph was sold into slavery when he was seventeen years old. He was thirty years old when he became Egypt's viceroy. Estimates of his time in prison range from seven to nine years.

6 By focusing on Black male incarceration, this essay in no way aims to diminish the fact that the incidence of Black females whose lives are tied up in the US prison system is on the rise and disproportionate to their percent of the population. See Michele Goodwin, "The New Jane Crow: Women's Mass Incarceration" Just Security, July 20, 2020, https://www.justsecurity.org/71509/the-new-jane-crow-womens-mass-incarceration/. In addition, Rodney Sadler reads the narrative of Joseph, which he identifies as the "Joseph novella." Sadler emphasizes the parallels between Joseph's brothers selling him into slavery with the selling of Africans by Africans to the European slave traders. See Rodney

Sadler Jr., "Genesis," in The Africana Bible: Reading Israel's Scriptures from Africa and the African Diaspora, Hugh R. Page Jr., ed. (Fortress Press, 2010.), 70–79.

7 See "Black Male Statistics," Black Demographics, https://blackdemographics.com/population/black-male-statistics/.

8 Miguel De La Torre, *Genesis* (Westminster John Knox Press, 2011), 300.

9 See William Shakespeare, *Othello*, 3.3.

10 Kathleen O'Connor, *Genesis 25B–50* (Smyth & Helwys Publishing, 2020).

11 Mary Lamia, "What Jealousy is Trying to Tell You," *Psychology Today*, June 26, 2020, https://www.psychologytoday.com/us/blog/intense-emotions-and-strong-feelings/202006/what-jealousy-is-trying-tell-you.

12 For insights on family life of ancient Israel see Michael Kruse, "Household: Family and Household in Ancient Israel," *Kruse Kronicle* (blog), June 20, 2007, https://krusekronicle.typepad.com/kruse_kronicle/2007/06/household-famil.html; also in reference to the privilege that the tunic with sleeves affords Joseph, see De La Torre, *Genesis*, 301.

13 De La Torre, *Genesis*, 301.

14 Lamia, "What Jealousy is Trying to Tell You," 2020.

15 O'Connor, *Genesis 25B–50*, 148.

16 For interpretations on how Joseph ends up being taken to Egypt, see O'Connor, *Genesis 25B–50*, 150.

17 Terence E. Fretheim, *The Book of Genesis: Introduction, Commentary, and Reflections* (Abingdon Press, 1994), 609.

18 Terence Fretheim ascribes Potiphar's wife's sexual advancements toward Joseph as indicating that Potiphar's sole attention to his economic prosperity, to which he accounted to Joseph's industry may have caused him to neglect the needs of his wife. This, with the fact that Joseph was "well built and handsome," could serve as the impetus for Potiphar's wife taking note of Joseph. Fretheim, *The Book of Genesis*, 609–10.

19 O'Connor, *Genesis 25B–50*, 168.

20 Ibid., 168.

21 Fretheim notes that Joseph being cast into prison was a lesser punishment than that required/expected. According to Israelite law his charge of attempted rape was to be met with death (Leviticus 20:10; Deuteronomy 22:22).

22 Fretheim, *The Book of Genesis*, 609–10

23 See "Crime and Punishment," *The Oxford Encyclopedia of Ancient Egypt*, Donald B. Redford, ed. (Oxford University Press, 2001).

24 "As of October 15, 2016, the National Registry of Exonerations listed 1,900 defendants who were convicted of crimes and later exonerated because they were innocent; 47% of them were African Americans, three times their rate in the population. About 1,900 additional innocent defendants who had been framed and convicted of crimes in 15 large-scale police scandals were cleared in 'group exonerations'; the great majority of those defendants were also black. Judging from the cases we know, a substantial majority of innocent people who are convicted of crimes in the United States are African Americans." Gross, Samuel R. et al., "Race and Wrongful Convictions in the United States," The National Registry of Exonerations (Newkirk Center for Science and Society, 2017).

25 This process of socialization within the prison entails following the prison code which consists of five key elements, or rules: Don't interfere with other inmates or tell on other inmates; Mind your own business; Don't whine or complain; Don't exploit other inmates, and always keep your word; Don't trust prison guards or staff. Laura Langford, "Prison Subcultures," https://study.com/academy/lesson/prison-subcultures-the-deprivation-model.html.

26 See "Prisoner Communications," *InsideTime*, accessed February 2, 2022, https://insidetime.org/prisoner-communications/.

27 Anita Stratos, "Perchance to Dream: Dreams and Their Meaning in Ancient Egypt," http://www.touregypt.net/featurestories/dream.htm.

28 For examples of ex-offenders becoming contributing members of society see "Can Ex-Prisoners Become Productive Members of Society?" *Prison Fellowship*, https://www.prisonfellowship.org/2018/04/can-ex-prisoners-become-productive-members-of-society/.

29 Christy Visher and John Eason, "A Better Path Forward for Criminal Justice: Changing Prisons to Help People Change," *Brookings Report*, https://www.brookings.edu/articles/a-better-path-forward-for-criminal-justice-changing-prisons-to-help-people-change/.

30 See Nelson Mandela, *A Long Walk to Freedom: The Autobiography of Nelson Mandela* (Time Warner Books, 1995).

31 See J. William Worden "Four Tasks of Mourning," in *Grief Counseling and Grief Therapy: A Handbook for the Mental Health Practitioner*, 5th ed. (Springer Publishing Company, 2022), 41–53.

32 As per the Egyptian laws of ritual purity, it was a common custom for Egyptians to abstain from eating with foreigners. See Genesis 43:32.

33 Harold Dean Trulear and Denise Strothers, eds., *Healing Communities USA Training Guide: Balancing Justice with Mercy* (Healing Communities, 2021), 45, Kindle.

34 United States Department of Justice, "Prisoners and Prisoners Re-Entry," https://www.justice.gov/archive/fbci/progmenu_reentry.html.

35 The survey defines close family members as "including parents; brothers; sisters; children; current spouse; romantic partner; step, foster, and adoptive family members." See Enns, Peter K. et al., "What Percentage of Americans Have Ever Had a Family Member Incarcerated?: Evidence from the Family History of Incarceration Survey," *Socius* 5 (2019).

36 Enns et al., "What Percentage of Americans Have Ever Had a Family Member Incarcerated?"

37 See Nazgol Ghandnoosh et al., "Parents in Prison," The Sentencing Project, https://www.sentencingproject.org/policy-brief/parents-in-prison/.

38 Ibid.

39 Ibid.

40 Veronica Crawford Lynch, "Facilitating Connectedness Between Families and Incarcerated Individuals," in *Ministry with Prisoners & Families: The Way Forward*, ed. W. Wilson Goode, Sr., et al. (Judson Press, 2011), 121.

41 Ibid.

42 "Criminal Justice Fact Sheet," NAACP, https://www.naacp.org/criminal-justice-fact-sheet/.

43 See John Bowlby, *Attachment: Attachment and Loss*, vol. 1, 2nd ed. (Basic Books 1982).

44 Wayne E. Oates, *Grief, Transition, and Loss: A Pastor's Practical Guide* (Fortress Press, 1997), 21–22.

45 Eric Martin, "Hidden Consequences: The Impact of Incarceration on Dependent Children," National Institute of Justice, March 1,

2017, https://nij.ojp.gov/topics/articles/hidden-consequences-impact-incarceration-dependent-children.

46 Goode, Sr. et al., *Ministry with Prisoners & Families*, v.

47 Keith Reeves, "Finding a Lazarus," in Goode Sr. et al., *Ministry with Prisoners & Families*, 46–47.

48 Lynch, "Facilitating Connectedness Between Families and Incarcerated Individuals," 126–27.

49 Ibid., 120.

50 See "7 Helpful Programs for Children of Incarcerated Parents," Connect Network, https://web.connectnetwork.com/programs-for-children-of-incarcerated-parents/.

51 See Oates, *Grief, Transition, and Loss*, 21-22.

52 For more information on the programming of this agency, see "Angel Tree," Prison Fellowship, https://www.prisonfellowship.org/about/angel-tree/.

53 Lynch, "Facilitating Connectedness Between Families and Incarcerated Individuals," 126–127.

54 See Chapter 15 in Goode, Sr. et al., *Ministry with Prisoners & Families*, 169–78; also see Trulear and Strothers, *Healing Communities USA Training Guide*.

55 Trulear and Strothers, *Healing Communities USA Training Guide*, 67–68.

56 Ibid., 67–68.

57 Harold Dean Trulear, "Changing Congregational Culture: The Healing Communities Model," in Goode Sr. et al. *Ministry with Prisoners & Families*, 169–70.

58 Ibid., 169–70.

59 Al Miles, *Domestic Violence: What Every Pastor Needs to Know* (Fortress Press, 2011), 104.

60 Trulear and Strothers, *Healing Communities USA Training Guide*, 62–63.

61 Ibid., 82.

62 Ibid., 82.

63 Ibid., 89–90.

64 Ibid., 90–91.

65 Ibid., 91–92.

66 Ibid., 92.

67 Raphael Warnock, "Lifting Our Voices and Liberating Our Bodies in the Era of Mass Racialized Incarceration," in *Black Practical*

Theology, ed. Dale Andrews and Robert London Smith Jr. (Baylor University Press, 2015), 271.

68 Emily Dufton, "The War on Drugs: How President Nixon Tied Addiction to Crime," *The Atlantic*, March 26, 2012, https://www.theatlantic.com/health/archive/2012/03/the-war-on-drugs-how-president-nixon-tied-addiction-to-crime/254319/.

69 As taken from Kirsten Weir, "Life on the Outside," *Monitor on Psychology* 46, no. 11 (2015): 67.

70 Gregory Ellison II, drawing upon the work of sociologist Christian Parenti, identifies two roles for Black disaffected youth within the dominant society: those who are considered social junk who have had their spirit crushed by societal pressures causing them to result to unhealthy coping mechanisms, and those who are considered social dynamite who continue to make themselves known usually in destructive ways. While his categories apply to young Black males, I see the possibility of these two terms being applied to many Black males who have been incarcerated and are now seeking to be reacclimated to society. See Gregory Ellison II, *Cut Dead but Still Alive: Caring for African American Young Men* (Abingdon Press, 2013).

71 The chapter title refers to a song by the Hollies, written by Bobby Scott and Bob Russell, originally recorded by Kelly Gordon, Capitol Records, 1969.

About the Authors

Editors

Reverend Raynard D. Smith, Ph.D.

The Reverend Dr. Raynard D. Smith is the Associate Professor of Pastoral Care/Pastoral Theology at New Brunswick Theological Seminary in New Brunswick, NJ, where he currently serves as Director of the Master of Arts in Pastoral Care and Counseling program. In addition, he is the Chair of the John Suydam Kuhlthua Bioethics Conference. He teaches courses in Pastoral Psychology. He has published two edited volumes, *With Signs Following: The Life and Ministry of Charles Harrison Mason* and It *Is Written: Minutes of the General Assembly Church of God in Christ Held at Memphis, Tennessee, 1919-1932*. Dr. Raynard Smith holds a Ph.D. in Psychology and Religion from Drew University; Masters of Divinity degree and Masters of Theology degree with a concentration in Pastoral Care and Counseling from Princeton Theological Seminary, and a Bachelor of Science degree in Biology and Religion from Springfield College. He is also an associate minister at Holy Mountain Church of God in Christ (COGIC) in Rahway, NJ, and co-founder and coordinator of the COGIC Scholars Fellowship, a network of seminarians and academics within the COGIC and other Pentecostal denominations. He is also a former member of the National COGIC Board of Education.

Reverend Terry Ann Smith, Ph.D.

The Reverend Dr. Terry Ann Smith is the Associate Dean of Institutional Assessment and Associate Professor of Biblical Studies at New Brunswick Theological Seminary. Dr. Smith oversees the assessment of the institution's degree programs, its certificate programs and the Lilly grant on Economic Challenges Facing Future Ministers. She teaches biblical Hebrew and courses in the Old Testament. Her writings include various articles on the book of Daniel, Rachel and Leah, Sarah and Ishmael, and the prophet Isaiah. She is currently co-authoring a commentary on Ezra-Nehemiah. Dr. Smith holds a Ph.D. and Master of Philosophy from Drew University in Madison, NJ, a Master of Divinity from New Brunswick Theological Seminary, and a Bachelor of Science in Management and Master of Science in Information Systems from Roosevelt University in Chicago, IL. She is an Associate Minister at Welcome Baptist Church in Newark, New Jersey.

Contributing Authors:

Reverend Micah McCreary, Ph.D.

The Reverend Dr. Micah L. McCreary is the president of New Brunswick Theological Seminary, New Brunswick, NJ. He teaches courses on race, class and gender at the masters and doctoral levels. He is an ordained minister in the Reformed Church in America and dually aligned with the National Baptist Convention of America and American Baptist Convention. Dr. McCreary has served in the pastorate of Baptist churches in Virginia. He has several years of experience as a clinical psychologist in private practice and professor of psychology at Virginia Commonwealth University in Richmond, Virginia. Dr. McCreary has a Master of Science and a PhD in counseling psychology from Virginia Commonwealth University, a Master of Divinity degree from the Samuel DeWitt Proctor School of Theology at Virginia Union University and Bachelor of Science degree in Engineering from the University of Michigan in Ann Arbor, Michigan.

Janice McLean-Farrell, Ph.D.

Dr. Janice McLean-Farrell is the Dirk Romeyn Assistant Professor of Metro-Urban Ministry and Assistant Dean of Doctoral Studies at New Brunswick Theological Seminary. She teaches in the areas of urban ministry, research methods and community leadership and conducts research in the areas of religions of the African Diaspora, Christianity in the Caribbean, migration, urban immigrant youth and religion, immigrant churches in the Diaspora, marriage and sexuality among Black immigrant youth in NYC; and women and migration. Dr. McLean-Farrell has a Ph.D. in Divinity from the University of Edinburgh, Edinburgh, UK, Master of Theology from Princeton Theological Seminary, a Master of Divinity from Gordon Conwell Theological Seminary; and a Bachelor of Arts degree from the University of Delaware.

She is the author of numerous articles and books, including *West Indian Pentecostals: Living their Faith in New York and London* (Bloomsbury, 2016).Dr. McLean-Farrell serves on the steering committee of the World Christianity unit of the American Academy of Religion, co-chair of the Religion and Education section of the Mid-Atlantic Region -American Academy of Religion, and she is a member of the Vital Worship Grant Advisory Board for the Calvin Institute of Christian Worship at Calvin College.

Reverend Fulgence Nyengele, Ph.D.

Dr. Fulgence Nyengele is Professor of Pastoral Care and Counseling in the William A. Chryst Chair in Pastoral Theology and Director of the Doctor of Ministry and the M.A. in Counseling Ministries programs at Methodist Theological School in Ohio (MTSO). He is also Director of MTSO's Thriving in Ministry Initiative, funded by the Lilly Endowment. An ordained elder in the United Methodist Church, he served United Methodist congregations in Southern California and was a staff pastoral counselor at the Clinebell Institute of Pastoral Counseling at Claremont, California, prior to joining the MTSO faculty. A native of the Democratic Republic of Congo, he is a member of the American Academy of Religion, the Association of Clinical Pastoral Education, and the Society for Pastoral Theology. Dr. Nyengele has also lectured and offered seminars and training for clergy and other ministry workers in Germany, Burundi, South Africa, and the Congo on topics as varied as ministry leadership in a multicultural world, theological education in the global context, spirituality for pilgrims, strangers and exiles, family systems theory in pastoral ministry, trauma and resilience, and pastoral care and counseling. His teaching and research are undergirded by a concern for relational wholeness and human flourishing, and his current research is exploring theories of human flourishing as expressed in the African tradition of Ubuntu and the relatively new movement of positive psychology.

Acknowledgments

We would like to express our deep gratitude to everyone who supported us during the creation of this book from its inception to its publication. This project would not have been possible without the contributions of many individuals and institutions.

We are especially grateful to Dr. LL DuBrieull whose initial feedback on the manuscript set the stage for this work's progress towards completion. We thank Dr. Paul Kim for his invaluable feedback and assistance throughout the early phase of the research and writing process. We extend our sincere thanks to Katie Martin and The Pilgrim Press for their ongoing commitment and support of this effort and thanks to Diane Hackenberg for helping shape our ideas into the final manuscript. We owe a debt of gratitude to our colleagues, Dr. Micah McCreary, Dr. Janice McLean Farrell, and Dr. Fulgence Nyengele, who when asked to contribute to the project responded affirmatively. We express our appreciation to Dean Beth Tanner for her support throughout the process of bringing this book to fruition. We are also grateful to our colleagues at New Brunswick Theological Seminary and especially to all our students who read parts of the manuscript and offered critical feedback. This work is dedicated to them as future pastors and leaders.

On a personal note, we would like to thank our families and friends, whose patience, love, and encouragement kept us grounded during this journey. Your support made all the difference.

Lastly, we would like to express our heartfelt thanks to our readers, especially those serving in Black Churches, who work tirelessly to bring hope to their congregants. We also extend our gratitude to those in the Academy, whose contributions enrich our understanding and growth. We hope this book inspires and informs their ministries and works in ways we have envisioned.